brief

thoughts

to

mull

before (or after)

you

vote

Contents

DA BAIT

It happened. But what was it?

When it was is clear. It was Wednesday, 9 EST on several stations.

TV stations, and probably the sound was broadcast on radio too.

First there was friendly handshake-greetings and male-bond-type mutual touchings of shoulders. Then the two candidates for the next Presidential term stood at their separate podia (or would it be podium -- "separate" denotes individual, singular: podium. But that doesn't sound right. Then how about "each stood at <u>his</u> separate podium"? Eh, who cares other than me!-I?)

Who else cares. The candidates' frequently overridden moderator, beyond and somewhat below their stage level almost like a "prompter" for a Shakespearian or operatic presentation . . . . was in his place. And the amount of time Mitt and Barack exceeded allocated durations despite attempted moderator interruptions and scoldings was pretty much equal.

Both parties of both Parties seemed respectful, almost congenial, and at times humorous inclusive of subtle self-deprecation.

No troublesome subjects were brought up or thrown (up to throw) at either of the . . . .contenders? . . . .

There was no mention of American Extremist Fundamentalist Phobias and paranoias: Mormonism being an a-Christian (if not, to some, anti-) cult. Not a word about Mormon Mitt.

There was no mention of the "flat-earther"-analogous fringe beliefs that Obama is an illegal alien (if not in his capacity of U. S. resident, in his position as President in that that specifies the occupant be of American birth. I'm sure there are some amongst some -- though not <u>us</u> -- who would attribute his proof of "citizenship/birth-cert." to Satan . . . . analogous to their asserting that anthropological fossils of "intermediate species" -- thus evidence of evolution -- were put where they were found by the devil.

As well as Obama cartoonified with a Hitler moustache, I've seen him depicted with diabolic horns and tail!! etc. in Internet stuff -- proof enough to some who know from other infallible (Biblical) source, too, that Beelzebub was not born in the United States of America.

There was hardly mention that the whole economic situation was the result of a "systemic pre-existing condition" and that at least Obama's administration has maintained a stability of (actually accomplished a slight ascent from) debacle.

There was scant mention of immigration, none of military guy-gays.

Both Mitt and Barack presented excellent appearance, admirable behavior, and constrained contexts of what they considered, thus what they . . . conversed about . . . . ?.

There was no mention of gaffes such as Mitt's "48% or Barack's "clinging to guns and religion". Neither Mitt's "not concerned about the poor" nor Barack's "didn't do it yourself", both statements obviously taken out of context and expanded to *absurdum* almost as if issues.

No mention of Guantanamo, closing it the quest to revive Constitutionality (such as *habeas corpus* and due process). Too bad pervasive lack of hospitality resulted in no alternative venues in which to house the horrific (but as well, how many innocents just caught up in the chaos not wedded to it as actual terrorists, but sold to the coalition for some bribe-price to a tribal adversary?) That wasn't brought up as an Obama "broken promise" or "failure"

There was hardly personal *ad hominem.* Mitt could have mentioned Obama's "clinging-to-guns-and-Bibles" remark. Worse, about his inept bowling earning him a "Special Olympics score" ,or something to that effect. (Truly a thoughless analogy from the President of the country!! Various very pejorative critiques could be made of the reference: the "inferiors", relative to the referencer, Harvard unto Chief Executive, etc.). There was no mention of Romney's realm of almost obscene privilege (elevator for the car in one of the estates) -- the hardly proportionate-to-necessity "physical therapy equipment" for Mrs. Romney: $100,000 horse, dressage ring, stable, paddock, no doubt groom.

No mention.
No snide remarks.
No innuendo.
No taunts.
Not even put-downs.

Debate? More like a conversation took place on that stage last Wednesday at 9PM. A friendly conversation. There was no evident impatience, exasperation, annoyance, anger, and except for the few instances of humor (which both seemed to appreciate as humorous), ... nothing emotional.

Interruptions (futile to constrain running over time limits) and essentially ignored admonitions (from a mere PBS guy to the President and the multi-multi-millionaire) were made with self-effacing good humor too. The runnings-over were solely for a candidate to continue his statement to a necessary state of completion. Otherwise the "hanging-<u>chat</u>" (incomplete presentation of premise or policy) might function as "preemptive hanging chad" -- eventual votes lost due to incomplete information from candidate.

Except for perhaps two very brief incidences, I don't remember any overlap or attempted over-riding of "the floor". For the overwhelming most- part, Mitt completed his say, then Barrack had his, and vice versa. Little talking over, butting-in, gesticulating, gyrating. It seemed each was a respectful audience of the other.

The decision to have the audience itself remain silent, which it did (except for a couple instances of very subdued laughter), was wise. No "gallery gallimaufry" of sounds to . . . . de-dignify . . . the . . . . *debate*??

If other than conversation, it truly seemed more like a presentation of projected policies (by Mitt) and review of achievements (by Barack). And these presentations were equivalent to what one would expect of very-upper level corporate officers presenting to the board as differentials, not adversaries.

But perhaps my perception of such professional and almost fraternal format was warped. Like, maybe, the on stage waters weren't as quiescent as it seemed to me. Maybe there was a factor such as when one witnesses a mere storm surge, it seems placid after he's been immersed in a veritable maelstrom for media-months, more like a tsunami of unending and unlimited reciprocal trashings, heard on the broadcasts of ballistics of bullshit of the campaign. In comparison, the stage- personal appearances were, relatively, pristine and poised. Yes, the term "dry" would apply.

But cordial, though maybe not quite convivial. . . . although seeing the co-mingling of Romneys and Obamas at the end, I wouldn't be surprised if they all headed off together for a great dinner and fine wine, then maybe to one of Mitt's mansions for an overnighter prior to their having to get on to their stumps and stances on the morrow. I can picture at least the younger of Mitt's boys challenging Barrack's girls on some video game while the parents perused, amused, the news reviews. (Though only one of the men uttered "whew!!"s).

For even in the PBS "playback" *immediately* after the event, along with the two women correspondents, the two men (one representing the NY Times, and I forget the older jowly guy's affiliation) opined that Mitt had "won". There was wonder if Barack was "rusty" from not having recently debated.

And I wondered if such, perhaps "catalyst" for other "grading-reportage" was actually a Democratic Party "strategy" for opinion. Yes, I'm off in the conspiratorial deep end here. But from what I watched, "debate" didn't really fit. And the specifics, the components of "the debate" seemed almost ultimately removed from evaluative juxtaposition. And I'll move on to the next paragraphs to explain what I mean.

I'm not providing any extent of play-by-play here. I'm giving my overview/summary of what I saw and heard. A transcript of everything said would provide extensive examples of what I'll just touch on.

Barack "recited" his accomplishments, though without going into much detail. During his administration oil drilling, though below all-time highs, had increased. The unemployment rate, though still unacceptably high, had been brought down a bit. Institutions of crucial finance and manufacture were sustained (after Bush's initial "bail outs" as resuscitation). And there were several other areas that Barack presented as his administration's accomplishments.

Mitt by no means refuted, actually hardly challenged, any of the above.

I'm surprised that Obama didn't bring up the brought-up (to dangerously implosive levels in my estimation) -- the stock market during his term. (Oh god, let's hope it wasn't because he knew enough not to wave a bubble as a banner).

Yes, as well, both candidates stated several matters which resulted in disagreement unto denial.

One matter was that a Romney win would result in very unfair tax breaks/advantage for the very upper echelon. I don't recall that specific percentages or other statistics were given. Mitt denied that his campaign had ever said such a thing. It seems that at some point he stated, almost as a correction of misconception, that he advocated no tax breaks, but he would provide tax advantages in order to stimulate the economy/job-growth.

To this there was hardly rebuttal from Obama. "Break?" "Advantage?" Newspeak nuance??

An obverse concerned the effects of "Obamacare". Romney, without any details other than some agency "finding" (not his exact words) said that it would seriously and deleteriously increase health costs. Obama cited his side's "findings" that the result would be a significant savings for the lower income demographic, and, of course, expanded coverage for those who now have insufficient or no health insurance. Overall, Obamacare would save money.

Were it so simple, one or the other of the candidates was either basing information on misinformation, erroneous calculations, or conducting calculated misrepresentation of the actual financial-facts.

Obviously it's not so simple and, given the nature of statistics, both diametrically opposed extrapolations might be "true". Or neither. Or vice versa. But neither Mitt nor Barack pursued any depths of this area. That national health care had originated as a Republican platform issue was just touched by Barack. That Mitt had, (a state-level mini-mirror-image of the Obamacare resistance) managed to establish what I'd love to see called "Romney-care" as Massachusetts' government-regulated system . . . . was just mentioned, not "used" by Barack.

Both men seemed in agreement regarding improving education. Mitt asserted (more than once) that during his governorship Mass. schools had became the highest achieving in the nation. I don't have any notes to refute, but it seems that's not what I've read here or there. Obama did not even question Mitt's claim to high-scoring-scholastics fame.

To that point (rather, within the scope of considered contexts up to then), there seemed to be not a draw, but just a two-part presentation of their accomplishments (as President by Barack), and as governor (and businessman by Mitt).

A brief review up to this point:

Barack's presentation was to point out his accomplishments and his side's conclusions (though not evidence per se) concerning what a Romney administration would produce, entail, incur, but not unto *inflict*! Mitt's response was not a retort or refutation, let alone outright denial except for alleged amount of "tax break for the rich" regarding which he asserted, "I never said that". Barack let any contestation go except for a comment about Mitt now ("I never said that") not being the Mitt then who did say that. Wise strategy.

Focus on factuality (even questionable) puts anything personal in the periphery. Trying to nail Mitt on ,(if it was) "denial" or "deviousness, might have been seen by the electorate as an attack-overcompensation for Obama's vulnerability!! Or as uppity-arrogance.

Another "persona-perspective" occurred to me concerning demeanors.

Dignity, even "somewhat stilted", is dignity compared to what a "loosened-up and 'got-down' " Barack Obama would personify in the racial-lens of so many. Even if not an actual performance, agile or argot, of the first "black" man to be President of the United States. Obama's white-ish presence was probably based on very careful considerations that any"blackishness" would be a serious blemish. Racism is regionally rampant still.

"Rusty from not having debated?" I return to that for a second.

Well, in a non-debate there was hardly opportunity for debate without (especially) someone being seen as arrogant, or elitist or controlling, . . . or out of his place. So, again, Obama was a polished presenter of his party's position, its assumption of accomplishments, and tactful, intended "factual" refutations of the other side's stance or statements in cases.

Yes, Barack was almost out-of-character controlled, staid. Compare to his speech at the Boston convention back almost four years ago. Compare to other presentations of his charisma, inspiring elocution. Compare to his campaign comments the day following the "debate" . . . . concerning Romney and the
"wild-card" (not Obama's term) tax rebate/advantage amount for the uppers!!

As for Mitt?

To use the term, *"channeling",* may be an ultimate "concatenation of disjoint" -- meaning that such a "new-age" idea applied to right-wing Conservatism . . . might even be explosive -- or cause spontaneous dematerialization of concept! Lurid liberal times ultra-right equals zero?

But watching Mitt, smiling, energized, if not actually gesticulating (somewhat vertically brachiating), seeing his animation, amiability and all . . . . I couldn't help but wonder if he was actually *"channeling the Gipper".* Either that or with coaches he'd been rehearsing his Reagan impersonation and got it down to subtle perfection more effective than anything more copy-cat blatant.

But maybe I just "saw-in", read-in "concatenation of similarity" (my extrapolated, or imagined, linkage but a systemic of epiphenomenal unrelateds).

Or something like that.

Focusing on Reagney (whoops, I mean Romney), can we deny having seen a transformation, a transmutation, a metamorphosis (from the wearying worm of so much editorial critique of his "dullness", etc.) . . . now this glorious flight (arms aquiver with enthusiasm) of the "better fly" (with him than with the "bumbling Beerack", Obama).

Reagan-routing or not, Mitt's animation, especially toward the conclusion of the affair, was effective, although it seemed to me a bit affected. Like, this isn't the "real Mitt". Kind of a Wendy's-ad thing, where it was almost like "good ol' Dave Thomas" chattin' (even after he lost so much weight he'd gained maybe eating so much of what his restaurants serve). "I'm-jus'-one-of-you-people-so-come-sit-with-me-at-my-table-Dave." From things I've read here or there, including a statement by one of his sons, it seems he was really a very hard-driven, hard-driving Type-A.

And all along for months, the Mitt seen on the stump-stops was not the Mitt seen on the stage where he pulled it off so admirably, animatedly.   Behaviorally. I found myself thinking that Barack Obama appeared so "Waspish" . . .and Mitt was almost "grooving' to and with *his* rap." Though I don't think I discerned any actual cadence.

Other than regarding tax breaks/incentives? and a couple other "line-items", Barack really took no issue with what Mitt mooted. Again, they agreed on improving/enhancing education, Barack specifying his desire to hire 110,000 teachers (to pay with what? -- a question that Mitt didn't pursue.)

At the "contextual point of the 'debate' " I've reached in this discussion, I felt that equivalent validities of presentation and points thereof had taken place.

A TIE!, if we're going to score a non-game, a non-contest.

For I didn't see it as a debate. If I spent the time to look up "debate" and compare all the facets and factors and components and complexities of this *"binary format of juxtaposition-for-evaluative-conclusion"* . . . . (wha . . okay, yes, that does make sense . . . .) if I really studied "debate", and compared, in detail and dynamic, what took place last Wednesday at 9 PM EST, I'm sure I'd be comparing apples to . . . . guys. Two men taking turns having their say.   For there was no real juxtaposition, discreditation of data or declaration, etc. etc. etc. No rebuttals, retorts, refutations, retaliations, or the rest of repertoire that made debates of the past demi-dramatic demonstrations. This time it was simply declarations.

Two guys in suits on a stage behind podia (-ums?) before/above the "moderated moderator" from PBS (who I'm sure was careful because especially some one of Romney's companies might become a significant contributor to programming since federal funds to provide chamber music and opera to the teeming masses have been so drastically cut-off. (In my nano-contributory way, I make up for some of what the trusts and estates and corporations don't completely cover to keep the classics coming to me . . . while the curtailed Fed funding is allocated to *needs* such as health or housing perhaps. Access to the arts (such as classical music) provides for the *wants* of the "aestheticarchy" or "aestheticocracy", ***artistocrats***? Yet everyone can tune-in to listen or watch, if not attend cultural events. But it's somewhat an "elitist-minority" who are into what PBS provides. PBS should be private enterprise and private persons or other payments provide for it.

But I must not digress further, for it's getting late.

I'm not sure how far from being done with this diatribe/dissertation I am.

I really want to finish it tonight, for I have much reading to do tomorrow, some of which will no doubt cover areas on which I'm writing now, and which I may wish, thus, tomorrow, that I'd waited until tomorrow to write what I'm writing about rather than tonight. Eh, I can always insert text, can't I?

It's getting late.
I must be getting to . . . . . . where was I????

Da Bait. Yes. DA BAIT.
What the hell does that mean?
Well, on the one hand it's obvious that it's a play-on-spelling of "debate".
But it's also a semi-homonym-ic transition of "debate" (discourse) to **"the bait"**, that which will attract and perhaps result in complete consumption of the candidate's presentation, (hook, line, and sinker) . . . by the voter.
Da Bait. The bait. That which at least gets the attention of the prospective catch, the voter. That which is cast upon the waters of the campaign, turgid, turbulent, or tastefully calm, really or relatively. Da Bait. That which may be swallowed whole by enough for the fisher of votes to mount unto the Washingtonian throne.
Obama's bait? It was his "this has been accomplished while I've been President. Like the configuration of a hook, here the focus turns "upon itself" as its field of consideration. Without refutation or dismissal by Mitt, one can assume that what Barack said was done . . . was done. And the "barb" of the hook of his bait may actually be that *the American people* are primary in his program of direct disbursements -- not the American Capitalists whose primacy, thus tax-related benefits, or perpetuation thereof, are supposed to result in jobs, thus payrolls, thus tax bases, thus government solvency, thus programs and progress for the masses (the perks of the masters totally above/beside the point). If not "channeling the Gipper", Mitt surely channeled "trickle down". He used a rather clever phrase, castigating Obama's alternative to Reaganian "trickle-down" (from private enterprise profit) . . . . "trickle-down government" as despicable, creeping-socialistic alternative.
(Mitt didn't allude to socialism, but I believe my words say what he would have.)
As for Mitt's bait?
His summation segment stated it in sequence of points he considered. Which I'm not replicating as a continuum here. But along with some of his points I will present my commentary.
Mitt stressed the importance of education, implying (at least) his role, if not responsibility/accomplishment, in elevating the level of Mass. schools.

> But I don't remember his detailing any federal program to thus
> enhance the nation's schools other than providing from Fed $
> to the individual states to administer and distribute to schools.

He acceded to the importance of health, care and costs, improvement and control, respectively.

> But his promulgation is, again, a state-administration, provided

with Fed funding. Mass's "Romneycare" is a state system. Mitt somewhat chided Barack for "forcing" Obamacare via "unfair uni-partisanship" -- as opposed to Mitt's supposed "crossing the aisle" for bipartisan enactment. That Mitt cited some supposed "confraternity" between Tip O'Neil and Ronald Regan involved, stirred a bit of mirth from the commentators. It seems that between Tip and Gip there was no love lost (how Fed funding approval for the "Big Dig" was forced thru Congress is fascinating . . and had stirred Reagan's comment, "I haven't seen so much lard since I judged a prize pig contest at a Kansas fair" (apprx. words).

Mitt noted being in favor of developing alternative energies.

His one "semi-*ad-hominem*" concerned the off-shoring of Evergreen Solar, the bankruptcy of Solyndra, and mention of a couple others. Mitt's mention that Osama's "investments" were into losers was "debatish" but, more, devious. And Obama's non-rebuttal, though perhaps strategized, might have lost points he'd have scored had he pointed out that 1) the very bastions of business and industry had either departed our shores or defaulted thereon . . .and 2) Mitt's contention -- that Fed$ Obama had put into these failed alternatives ventures could have financed pay for X# of teachers . . . is in a sense a senseless nonsequitor. Any attempt finance alternative energy is valid.

That we invest in alternatives is of strategic importance unless we just don't give a crap about our great-grandchildren and beyond. That some of those start-ups don't survive may reveal more the faulty Fed Govt. (compared to other countries as in Europe (surely not just China) where subsidies support experimentation and development of alternative energies until they hopefully become self-sustaining, even profitable).

Mitt mentioned clean coal. He's in favor of that as a major energy resource. Great for the very minor constituency who mine (or strip) coal. Great for assuring their votes.

But what about the environment, including atmos-phere, in the couple generations(?) duration until the seams' and decapitated mountains' yield run out?? But coal is bait for coal miners. And mine owners. Yet how small the employment-demographic, thus voter numbers.

Another matter in Mitt's bait-shop -- oil drilling. Flat out he stated he favors drilling in Alaska and on the continental shelves. More than bi-part bait here. For one thing, oil companies and personnel must have been instantly hooked hearing that proclamation.

And this gets me into several sub-areas of concern,.

First, just how many unemployed people does Mitt think he'll get back working by providing for more drilling, on- or off-shore? How many run a rig? I should look it up so as to cite data, but it's already a bit later than when I mentioned it getting late before. So let me "guesstimate". 500 total involvement per rig? So let me venture that we could put into pumperation a thousand rigs. That would give jobs to 500,000 people. Out of how many millions (+/- 8% of the population now unemployed . . . . .!?!?!?)

Second, I'll just mention the potentials for disaster. Each rig may represent (as a respected friend of mine stated it) a "small footprint". But as I replied unto him, citing Valdez and the little burbling miss-hap by BP, petro-drilling footprints sometimes bleed profusely!!

Third, who in his right mind would expect that more oil pumped out of anywhere is going to lower gas prices here (or anywhere) to @$2 per gallon? If one has adequate information (which I have but smatterings of) he realizes that it's almost that the oil companies are governments unto themselves. And their prices and profits are surely not "consumer-driven" (supply and demand) -- for they can diminish their supply (due to increased automotive efficiency or decreased consumption of product due to mobile curtailment -- people traveling less) and maintain "windfall profits" just by pumping-up pump prices! ExxonMobil and the others don't only have a cushion to protect them from any and all of anything . . . . they have a trampoline!!!

Fourth, As for OPEC, our "dependence" on their oil is far from threatening. From Canada come our primary petro-imports. And regarding OPEC itself, if we suddenly said, "screw you guys, we're outta here", how long would it be before those swarms of Saudi princes would be smothered by insurrection, and in the brutality of The Brotherhood or Alqaida or Martyrs or myriad other jihadis who would thus be unleashed from the West's militari-economic tethers of restraint? Our proxy-princes . .

Fifth, petro-input from wherever isn't always allocated to specific distribution. It seems there's kind of a "global pool" drawing from Africa, America, Canada, Caribbean, Chile, Norway, Mideast, Russia, Venezuela, and many elsewheres. One example of the "dispersion" is that, from what I understand, the majority of oil we pump out of America gets exported!!! Via the "collective pool".

Sixth. Does it really make sense to exploit our proven reserves (of anything -- even, or especially, if it lowers consumer prices) in order to stimulate even more usage of an ultimately finite resource? Even with the expense of trial-and-error (invest-but fail) interim of economic allocations, isn't R&D toward functional alternatives (especially "self-sustaining" such as solar, wind, wave) preferable to diminishing what we have but is non-replenishing??

It seems, without actual statistical analysis, that there would be far more jobs created in creating completely new systems, than those few people put back to work on oil platforms, mining or fracking facilities, etc.

And if, in a few generations, the US, in part thanks to Mitt, has depleted its "conventional" (oil/gas) resources, what then??

Perhaps we'll be so much less dependent upon "foreign energy" sources when we have none left? Would the neo-OPEC with headquarters in Sharia City extend philanthropic pipelines and and shipping lanes from their shores to ours? Would the energy cartels of any country then say unto America, "you tried so hard, you conserved so much, your people went without . . . . how can we now help you out with a somewhat Marshall-plan-ish provision of what we've preserved???

Still sixth: employment opportunities will result from new devices, systems, installations, not just the alternative energy sources. It would seem that Federal investment would be in such as priority.

Wind-solar and later other sources to supply
LED lighting via even separate building circuits
(though interfaceable with the conventional Grid).
Collection of and separate plumbing systems to

recycle "gray-water" for non-potable use (such as for toilets, industrial processes, etc. Knowing that water supplies are in drastic decrease (factoring population increment and deglaciation) . . . . to use pristine H2O in which to piss and shit is . . . . unconscionable!! (Also consider that we can ship Coke and Pepsi etc. all over the globe but millions have limited access to any water, and most of it unsafe!!

On-site housing (condos on office-park-campus expanses, even on all those acres of flat roofs), would not only put an awful lot of people to work (who wouldn't want to or be able to work on the oil rigs -- which wouldn't be able to employ them all anyway) . . . . . . and think of the commuting time and fuel consumption and pollution spew saved if one's commute to work would be but a few minutes' walk!!! (How well I know!!!) .

Instead of the daily miles and miles of creeping-hour (rush?) migration.

Yes, I could keep on going with categories of innovation and thus, as well as ecological benefit (or salvation), broad economic advantage even beyond job creation.

But enough. I hope I've made my point.

I felt that Mitt Romney's points were far from prodigious. Rather, they missed the points of what priorities should (and will have to) be. Except that as "bait", they were excellent. Mantras. Slogans. Drill, baby!! Petro-self-sufficiency!! Good ol' coal (so almost nostalgic). Domestic energy!!

One of Mitt's summation points was, "We can't keep going on the path we're on (referring to what Obama has really had no choice but to tread as his itinerary despite his best intentions.)

But Mitt's bait is based on everything, substantive and systemic, on which the errant and error'd path already taken has led us to -- where we're at!! *Laissez-faire* of the free-marketeers (business-boom based on credit/thus-deficit), banks bundling debt as if collateral compounding, overseeing agencies as ratings-sellers charging top price for the triple A. We've traveled that free-market path. States' rights as God's grounds for determinations -- thus such despicable disparates as health care, education, prison conditions, capital punishment criteria and on and on. You got Vermont and you got Alabama and you got Texas . . . . . . states . . . . deciding . . . allocating . . .

Obama's bait? His presentation of what he's accomplished against the "odds" of the outcomes of the gambles (and worse) of an administrations-continuum from before (inclusive of the S&Ls, the Greenspan bubble, the ongoing interim legacy costs overwhelming product-mediocrity of Detroit, the eventual outcome and realization of what seemed to Wall Street (global-"Wall Street") a profit bonanza of "securitizations" -- (the new "tulip" of profits).

Could Obama *have* done, could he do better? Better?

I think one of his statements was salient, concerning superseding partisanship regarding Obamacare. He said something to the effect that sometimes to lead, one has to just overcome by assertion (and, implied, even manipulation). But given "gridlock" there was only so much possible. And thus the protections of our government's "balances and checks" can result in . . . . checkmates??

Would Mitt do better? Mitt's proposals, his bait, will hook some. But they may find they're swimming the same submerged path which brought us to where we're at. Other than oil and coal, where will all those jobs come from?

He stated he was sick of paying money to China (apprx. words). Does he really think that it's a matter of China sucking off our economy -- which is our major manufacturing & marketing corporations!! (Walmart, for just one egregious example) so significantly profiting by doing business with/in China??. Even heavy, heavy industry profiting the US interests, dividends?

Doesn't he realize to what extent China's cheap labor is "an inverse input into *our* domestic economy" via that upper level demographic known as shareholders? Doesn't he realize to what extent American investment is in "Chinese" enterprise -- somewhat analogous to the "Japanese takeover" back some, what, 20 or more years ago? The Japs even bought Rockefeller Plaza!! Remember? Aghast, some bewailed and berated our "sellout". At exorbitant prices. Resulting in windfall profits for the sellers and even eventual re-possession of the defaulted and foreclosed properties when that market bubble busted and the Japs lost much for which they'd overpaid much.

Nobody's selling-out our own economic interests to China. We're exploiting China's economic interests.

But Mitt must have managed already to antagonize that massive, major populace and its leaders, prospering partner with us in globalism, but potential enemy if the "détente of economic symbiosis" were severed.

Will Mitt's bait actually provide any nutrient to those hooked? Not just, I might term it, "notion-nodules upon which to nibble?"

Ah, but perhaps the solution, the evolution of it all . . . . .
somewhat as the conclusion of projected-policy-presentation . . . . .
Mitt really enthused, **"we'll get that pipeline built"** . . . .

Will it be, "better a Biden"
 Or would you rather a Ryan?

or would the most mastery be by Martha?

,

Was it her "her-ness"? Female . . .

Such long hair and other features of her younger, probably exquisite beauty . . . still radiant . . .though matured.

So was it (too?) a "mother-image"? rather than just some old guy even positioned "beneath" Mitt and Barack. Last night this glowing, mature woman was on the same plane as (perhaps even higher *level* than) the guys in the VP show.

Though there were several instances of Ryan and Biden (especially the latter) interrupting, even persisting beyond his allotment while the other had begun his turn, even in these cases (of, I felt, childish impolitesse), it seemed she was in control -- allowing a little tussling, so to speak, but quite effectively putting a stop to it when she'd decided "enough too much" was enough.

Striking appearance: those high cheekbones somewhat suggesting "facial *broad shoulders*", thus strength, even power . . . . Was it by her "Valkyrie"-ness that Martha was able to curtail and control both the contestants so well? (In the third of the four-opera series *The Ring Cycle*, Brunhilde is the name of the leader of the Valkyries, the warrior women of the god, Wotan).

Martha Raddatz. The Brunhilde of the debate? For me to conflate her in any way with a Germanic, especially Wagnerian, character, may seem a juxtaposition far worse than the "*channeling the Gipper*" comment in my "Da Bait" essay. By the last name, I would assume Martha is Jewish. "German", in juxtaposition!?!?! . . . . especially when we bring in Richard Wagner who was one of the first to propound Jewish as ethnic. The Jew was no longer deficient and despicable due to the religion. It was his very *being* by heritage and "race". Thus, no longer possible was the "assimilation and salvation by Christian conversion. Jewish had become an incurable, unconvertible blood disease. There could be no "transfusion". Just, soon, *transport* due to Wagner's philosophy influential to Hitler's hate, not just the music to love.

Some time ago on some TV history thing I saw footage of Wagner's great nieces (?) and other relatives along on some outing or parade with him, and one holding Der Fuehrer's arm.

But to the debate.
Regarding Mr. Biden.

He made several semi-errors with facts and figures, words and terms. Most he caught and corrected immediately, including one comment involving the word "devastating" which his initial sentence seemed to be applying to the US's effect upon some situation abroad -- rather than the existing "devastating" situation itself -- which the US was attempting to resolve or ameliorate. I don't remember the specifics.

Biden's "ideational flow" had an interesting, somewhat distracting, pattern: the last word of a sentence would be, so to speak, over-ridden by the first word of his following sentence. The effect was "an abbreviation of terminal word" of a sentence, the meaning and intent of which was complete (at least in Joe's mind). So he thought no need for a "coda-word", so to speak -- a word after his stated completion of his thought. And so he'd get on with the next component of thought or thesis, the next sentence.

Interesting pattern. Usually this happens *between* people, one "coming-in" to dialogue as an overlap, a preemption of the other's completion. Biden's bipart barge-in is self-administered!

But I didn't find it deleterious to his, apparently, genuinely personal statements, actions, and interactions. This "spontaneity" spanned a spectrum from just looking and listening rather intently, to actions and reactions such as "what a bunch of crap!!! (he used the word 'baloney')". He laughed, almost scoffed now and then.

At times he became vehement, agitated, almost angry in response to Ryan. In these instances, it would appear that Biden was retorting with factual, documented, standpoints and information such as military chiefs-of-staff approval of, if not initial advocation of, Afghanistan draw-down -- also "ally" accord with US on deadline date. And there were a couple other issues.

Biden's grins, grimaces, and smiles, at times seemed almost, if not Tourettish, at least inappropriate, maybe silly, maybe supercilious. And there were at least two occasions when he protested to Martha that his opponent was having (especially for closing statement, might have) more time than he'd get. He sounded almost adolescent, bitching. Petulant.

Mr. Ryan's presentation was less interrupted by "instant self-corrections". But he, too, caught himself on fact or figure, a few times.

In significant contrast to Biden, Ryan's persona was a smooth, somewhat flattened continuum. My impression was that I was hearing and watching a meticulously rehearsed recitation and performance. Precise, and practiced. A speech -- without the spontaneity of statements (and certainly emotional and behavioral emanations) of Biden. No improvisation from Ryan.

The issue of foreign nations' loss of respect for America almost seemed a refrain, a *leitmotif,* played in several context-themes: failure to be more involved in Syria, not supporting Israel/Netanyahu sufficiently, proposed cuts to military. (I'll return to these matters below).

As with the Presidential debate, here in VP-land there were the stalemates.
R) Obamacare will cost billions and be deleterious.
D) Obamacare will save billions and be advantageous.

D) Enhancing, even just maintaining, tax cuts to the "rich" hurts the middle class & economy itself.

R) There will be no tax cuts, rather "relief" for the upper levels and this will allow investment into the economy to create jobs and help the middle class.

R) Raising business tax level will devastate small business owners, forcing them to close businesses.

D) Almost no small businesses owners make over $200,000 per year, thus the overwhelming majority of "business" will be unaffected by tax increase on the rich.

R) Cutting military budget will weaken America in the estimation of others

D) Military expenditure is excessive, in part going to provision of redundant or excessive (example given was tanks) equipment.

And there were a few other cases where the two sides were just contrary standpoints without any in-depth, or -breadth, examinations of situations and circumstances, documentation, data.

So, again on the VP level interaction, it was rather than a debate, it was more an "I say it's this way", "but I say that way", reciprocation of antitheticals really with no basis other than "platform" premise. No even purported *proof* within historical or contemporary context for the efficacy or wisdom of premises and platform positions.

Concerning what I said above that I'd return to . . . . .a number of concerns.
As above, R) is obviously for Republican premise, D) for Democrat.
1) Iran's nuclear program.
  SANCTIONS
  R) sanctions haven't stopped Iran enriching U, etc. Obama policy reveals
      weakness to stop Iraq's threat to develop nuclear bomb.
  D) sanctions are working and will eventually force the Mullahs to
supersede militaristic ambitions in order to sustain their theocratic
      positions from eventual popular insurrection (obviously my words here
      for what Biden was presenting as the Administration's rationale and
      assumption that basis its sanction policy).

There was no "rebuttal question" to Ryan such as, "had Romney been President, what would he have done heretofore. **Specify**. If Romney is elected, what will he do, assuming that Iran's actions and intents will not be altered just because of an administration change in Washington. **Specify**. What steps would a Romney presidency take, what actions? Criticizing Obama's alleged ineffectuality is far from a statement of intent, plan, platform.

The Obama administration's steps and actions are obvious -- existing policies and procedures. *De facto,* so to speak, if not by universal international acceptance of their validity, by overwhelming majority of concerned nations, the present paradigm is deemed the wisest course of action -- no preemptive military action, even to (try to) destroy Iran's facilities (a la Saddam's back some time ago). And it seems that if Israel decided to do so as last resort or preemptive self-defense, it would go ahead even in actual abrogation of its agreements, and violation of relationship, with US. What, pray tell, would the US do about it? Disown Israel? The West Bank building boom should be seen as an example of Israel doing what it will do regardless!

The threat of igniting the *whole* Middle East by "a fuse of fusillade" (so to speak) vs. Iran was cited by Biden, with references. Would greater respect for, perhaps fear of, the US be engendered by staging a "second act of Iraq", but this time not with an outcast outlaw (the semi-secular Saddam, hardly aligned with, rather, primarily despised by, his contiguous nations)? Would Islam-extremist rage (and retaliation) be rendered less threatening?

Perhaps especially to Israel?? Stuck there in the middle . . . of potential suicide-bomber *populations*?

I see Iran, or any other, unlikely to become a "suicide bomber <u>nation</u>." No doubt there's full awareness that if it did launch anything serious against Israel, Iran would be "obliterated" by the retaliation of a large coalition. Iran isn't hard to locate -- whereas terrorist *individuals* are just that, without populations and agendas and factions and financial enterprises and amassing of wealth and interests in survival for themselves, their families, their investments, and all.

A preemptive attack on Iran would, of course, be judged as primarily Israel's action (though US backed). How much greater the rage, thus individual terrorism the more stirred to wipe the Israel off the map if it actually enacted destruction on Iran!!! How "contained" and "confined" in source and system is Israel's water supply (for example). How much greater the existential threat to the country and its people . . . . after preemption on Iran . . . . thus unknown, unmonitorable individuals with little vials of virals in their attache cases . . . . or even shoved up undiscoverable places of person as they perused Tel Aviv before pouring into its pipes.

Perhaps some of these considerations should have been brought out by Biden?

But if time constrained, again, should he not have cornered Ryan by demanding, "Just what would a Romney administration have done to this point? And what will it do if elected?? SPECIFY!!!!!!"

One of Biden's points with brief but comprehensive backing information concerned Iran's stage with enrichment, vs. when it might have a weapon in which to put the stuff. Ryan didn't contest Biden's references. But Ryan should have picked up on the "no where near having a weapon". What happens if nothing happens to change the escalation, now just enriching? Somewhat a convoluted analogy to using up our resources until . . . WHAT

NOW . . seemed Biden's post-ponement of concern about Iran developing a nuclear weapon for its nuclear fuel. Maybe a bit of a ways off. But time passes. And . . .WHAT THEN???

Ryan should have ordered, "Specify!! When then -- whenever?"

WITHDRAWAL

R) Obama policy of set-date withdrawal from Afghanistan gives notice to Alqaeda so they have time to prepare for re-takeover/re-insurgency.
(this obviously an approximation of Ryan's statement).

D) Withdrawal date set not by US alone, and provides time frame (and necessity's incentive) for Afghan troops we've trained for that purpose to take over responsibility for their own country.

Biden did mention that to draw down such a theater as Afghanistan requires extensive time and logistics and coordination, so can hardly be contained until a "we're out of here, bye!" surprise.

And he could have further figured even if secrecy were attempted, leaks are unpreventable. The populace not being told in advance, thus "weaned" through a period of time, might see the US and allies as betrayers, devious, sneaks, and worse than even the other opinions they seem to have of us.

There were no considerations of whether our persistence is really defeating its very premise -- our attempted "advanced" democratization and modernization thus catalyzing the proportionate resistance by the very "socio-status" of the region (tribal, theocratic, misogynistic, and worse, to us -- but to them their valid reality).

Prior to Russia there were other lost-causes for some Western interests. Less under the guise of free-the-Iraqi-people "idealism" (our shtick) in *their* intention to secure routing of Mideast petro resources, Russia's actions in the area led to their withdrawal (by thwart, if not actual defeat).

US presence as an invasion, even defilement, of the Muslim realm is proliferated in public's perspective (propounded unto the populace from the pulpits of the Mosques). Another Crusade. An attempt to crush Islam -- as well as to superimpose (what we think of as progress and modernicity) our decadent immorality and materialism (which they, like our not-too-long-ago-Puritan-and-other-persuasion-forebears would, consider the sins of the Satanic!!)

Again, what would Romney have, or what will he do differently? SPECIFY!!

INVOLVEMENTS

R) Obama has not sufficiently provided support to overthrow Assad.
Weakness revealed by Russia and UN superseding US unilateralism (so

to speak) to enforce its national strength, accomplish its goals.

D) US has been acting within international contexts (again so to speak).

A President is not a dictator, either domestically or internationally. Within our system there are divisions of power, provision of checks and balances, veto, over-ride thereof. In very few cases can a President *Constitutionally* act alone. A final "contrarian decision" by Truman, to approve a Middle East Jewish state, defied the unanimous dissent of his whole cabinet. But even in this case there was the preceding "infrastructural" Congressional involvement.

Another situation was with the Bush/Cheney (and neo-con) con -- of Congress and others. This was a matter of mis-information (unto outright bullshit) by Bush and his little bunch. It led us into a multi-morass, billions debt serious, but insignificant compared to the loss of life, infliction of such suffering upon so many who managed to stay alive during the neo-"siege of Baghdad". And what, pray tell, was accomplished to strengthen our country, enhance the world's opinion of us, let alone others' *respect*?? We not only lost lives, we lost face!!

And prior, though we were justified in driving the Alqaeda-sheltering Taliban from power post 9/11 (we asked, and they could have turned Osama over), our continued involvement in Afghanistan accomplished what? At the cost of so many lives, for us to drive the militants out of their caves in the wilds of Afghanistan? Accomplished? There, logistics for their re-supplies were quite difficult for them. Communications, though, were very easy for us to monitor. But we cleansed them out, displacing them, no doubt, into the cities of Pakistan where vis-à-vis (no cell phones necessary) they could plot their plans and order their arms and huff their hookas totally unsurveilled!!

Our expunging the militants from the mountains of Afghanistan seems, to me, to have accomplished about as much as . . . . if during the roaring twenties the FBI had gone into the realms of Upstate New York and driven all the gangsters out of their getaways and conclaves. And when they'd all been "flushed" from the forests into the big cities of New York and Chicago, the Feds rejoiced, "We've solved the Mob Problem".

Regarding other areas of "involvements" . . . cases of sheer imposition by a nation, including ours, (without "weakened capacities" incurred by contexts and constraints such as UN, NATO, whatever) . . . . .

With Bush (*pere*) as head of CIA (and, interestingly, Kermit Roosevelt as primary operative and the father of Desert Storm Fame General Schwartzkopf in a major role, we surely got involved in Iran, overthrowing Mossadegh in order to reinstate the Shah (and Western control of interim-nationalized petroleum industry). And look what that led to rather soon. Hostages. Repressive religiosity. And the Iran of now!!!

How 'bout the "Arab Spring"? Western intervention primarily as incentive, approbation, cheering-on, maybe some weaponry, even a little air support . . . it seems that the overthrow of Libya's and Egypt's (like Iraq's) corrupt and cruel leaders has resulted in an expanded region and rule of "United Islam", truly A Brotherhood (and other titles of the factions/sects/divisions of the militants. And these represent a dispersion of direction now beyond our control.

The volatile vapor of a militant confraternity-unto-populace is a far worse threat than a contained pool of family or fanatic individuality, in spite of the corruption, even to some extent the cruelty. For let loose the rabid hordes, does not the carnage and cruelty just increase?? At least we could manipulate Khadafy, Mubarak, et. al.

It seems that the Romney-Ryan position is almost as criminally naïve as was the Bush-Cheney catastrophe regarding democratization of the Middle East through "controlled demolition of despotisms" -- Saddam as the fuse to set-off the regional chain reaction).

Regarding the regressive, repressive Saudis, what would Romney do? In ways, Saudi Arabia and its rulers represents a far worse scenario than many other places and personages. Think women's non-rights as just one example, Saudi Arabia in juxtaposition to, say, Turkey or even Iran!!! Wahhabism. Saudi support of terrorist organizations. Saudi origin of all but one of the 9/11 team. Etc.

It seemed that Biden should have nailed Ryan. What would Romney do?? SPECIFY!! About Assad? SPECIFY!!!! Make Syria and Iran the second of a double header firsted by Iraq??

Maybe that's the answer to the problems.
HAHAHAHAHAHA WIPEOUT!!!!
Scorched-earth policy. Neo-blitz firestorm finale of the whole wretched realm of regression and religion. Biblical!! With high-tech. Every man, woman, child, beast, and poison the fields to be ever-after barren.

And horrendous consequences, including that the enactment thereof would reveal the enactor as exponentially worse than those expunged by the explosives.

Would "regional genocide" be an ultimate Romney route? (Mormons for Armageddon?)
SPECIFY!!!!!

***

Iraq recent history

After WW II, America turned to the Middle East for petroleum supply. We established ally relationships with Saudi Arabia and also Iraq in order to secure our sources.

1987 Revolution in Iraq which turned toward Russia, also became anti-Israel. Us cools relationship and deals with Iran (overthrowing Iranian govt. which had nationalized their oil industry . .and we reinstated the Shah).

Iranian fundamentalist Islamic revolution. Our hostages taken and held for over a year. West realizes that Iraq not so bad as Iran.

1982 Iraq prepares for massive invasion of Iran . . springboard for a larger effort to thwart Iran's springboard of Islamic fundamentalism into other areas of the Middle East. American policy makers argue that Saddam is no different from other dictators American had worked with through the years. Iraq must be a defense against Iran.

America sides with Iraq. From 1982 through 1990, the U. S. policy is that "the enemy of my enemy is my friend". Reagan administration removes Iraq from its list of terrorist nations. So doing aids the

U. S. in supplying Iraq in its war with Iran (but we also supplied Iran with all kinds of strategic materials and weaponry and intelligence!!)

1983 Regan sends envoy to "make nice" with Iraq: Donald Rumsfeld. This was after the U. S. knew of Iraq's use of the U. N. banned mustard gas in the war. The U. S. State Dept. condemned Iraq's actions but took no punitive action.

1983 Reagan renewed actual diplomatic ties with Iraq the first time in two decades. After this, American support for Iraq increased -- involving critical information on Iranian troop movements. Agricultural credits were provided to Iraq to buy food from the U. S. so money could be allocated to the purchase of weapons from us. The extent of the agricultural economic-involvement was such that there was much lobbying for the maintenance of Iraq's approved status and recipiency.

Washington loosened control on the export of weapons and encouraged allies to do the same and "look the other way" when necessary. So all kinds of weaponry was sent to Iraq, thus contributing to the development of the "weapons of mass destruction" (which, before Gulf, Iraq possessed with our blessings). The U. S. contributions included selling Iraq strains of anthrax.

1987 campaign against the Kurds, many of whom had allied with Iran during war. Iraq uses poison gas. Indications of attempted genocide: 100,000 killed.

1988 U. S. Senate passes bill to punish Iraq. House waters bill down. Reagan administration kills it. Economic reasons are primary. In addition to the oil consideration, Iraq was the 2nd largest buyer of American agricultural products (second to Mexico).

1990 Iraq invades Kuwait. U. S. launches "Desert Storm", defeats Iraq in the desert, but also bombs Baghdad.

2003 Second Iraq war. Stated reason: to disarm weapons of mass destruction.

Misc. information regarding Saddam

His father died when he was a young boy,. He was sent to live with a relative who was abusive, and his interaction with neighborhood children was such that he was harassed as a "bastard".

Saddam lived with another relative in Tikrit. The person had been in prison for an attempted anti-British coup. Also, here Saddam was influenced by a culture of familial and tribal values which were the core of society and identification of the individual as well.

early 1950s   Saddam demonstrating against rich land owners.

1958   revolution overthrows British backed monarchy

1959   Saddam and Baathist fail in attempt to assassinate the Iraqi military leader. Saddam flees the country for four years.

1968   Saddam has returned and risen to power in Baath Party. Takes over security division, eliminates his rivals. On the basis of "Arab oil for the Arabs", money is put into schools, infrastructure, highways, etc. Lives of people are greatly enhanced. Baghdad becomes a cosmopolitan city.

1979   Saddam takes over presidency of Iraq. Videotaped purge of "traitors". Saddam on stage smoking cigar as supposed traitors' names are called out and they are led out, many to be killed.

1980   invasion of Iran ostensibly over a territory dispute concerning a waterway, and also due tot the Iranian fundamentalist revolution which Iraq (and the Western powers) wanted to keep from spreading. The eight-year Iran war killed more than a million people. The West supported Saddam against Iran.

1981   Iraq nuclear facility bombed by Israel. Saddam had stated, "The Iranian people should not fear the Iraq nuclear reactor . . .not meant to be used against Iran . . . .but against the Zionist enemy."

1988   end or Iran war. Billions of dollars of Iraq debts, Saddam wants cancelled.

1990   Iraq invades Kuwait, blaming West for stealing Iraqi oil (angle drilling)

1991   Saddam forced out of Kuwait. Baghdad bombed. Reported pinpoint accuracy of U. S. patriot missiles. Extensive looting by populace should have been precedent for what has happened now. But the only protection seems to have been given to the oil ministry building . . .while the mobs stole and destroyed everything else and U. S. military did nothing.

Brief history of Iran

1906   A constitutional revolution had taken place but was suppressed by the monarch, Ali Shah.

1907   Actual control of Iran was essentially divided between Britain and Russia

1908   Oil finally struck after numerous unproductive drillings

1909   Largest refinery in the world built at Abadan on Persian Gulf

1911   By then, pipelines were transporting oil out of Iran under the control

　　　　　　　　　　of Anglo-Persian Oil Company
　　　　　　　　　　British executives and other personnel lived in luxury
　　　　　　　　　　Iranian laborers subjected to horrendous saqualor
1920　　　Iranian royalty accepts British terms of 16% of net profits of Anglo
　　　　　　　　Persian Co (per an.), amounting to just L47,000 for one year.
　　　　Worldwide depression ensues and oil revenues decrease, thus royalties to Iran fall.
　　　　(As is now in the Middle
east, notably Arabia, the "pittance" payment from Western oil extraction entities
represented great luxury for the royalty and high-end few. But there was next to
nothing of benefit to the common masses.)
　　　　Social and economic conditions in Iran resulted in cancellation of the oil
concession to Britain. . . thus the necessity of Britain's renegotiating the agreement
up to L975,000 per an. and decreasing the size of the concession lands.

1941　　　Britain forces Reza Shah (the ruler responsible for the above) to abdicate
1945　　　Between '41 and '45, oil extracted increases from 6 ½ to 16 ½ mil. tons.
1948　　　Active in former nationalist movement but forced into exile by Shah for
　　　　　　　　20 years, Mossadegh elected to Majlis (like our Senate)
1950　　　Mossadegh became prime minister of Iran and was trying to negotiate
　　　　　　　　a 50/50 split of oil revenues with Britain
　　　　　　　　　　Britain absolutely intransigent in refusal
　　　　　　　　　　Mossadegh ultimately inflexible in compromise.

Mossadegh nationalizes Iranian oil industry and expels all British personnel. Britain sabotages Iranian Oil operations

　　　　　　　　Refuses visas for technicians answering ads for Iranian oil industry positions
　　　　　　　　　　and pressures other countries to do so
　　　　　　　　U. S. and Britain own 2/3 of world's oil tankers. Britain influences and U. S.
　　　　　　　　　　refuses any Iranian shipment of oil
　　　　　　　　Ship *Mary Rose* transporting Iranian nationalized oil seized by Britain.
　　　　　　　　　　Iranian exports of $45 million in '50 close to zero by '55
Prior Truman administration would not cooperate with Britain's colonialist intentions
regarding Iran. But Eisenhower came into office and went along with Churchill's agenda
providing U. S. (SSA renamed CIA) with authorization to overthrow Mossadegh and
reinstate the West-friendly Shah.
　　　　　　　　Coup against Mossadegh organized under George H. W. Bush's
　　　　　　　　leadership of CIA. Primary operative organizing mobs and handing]
　　　　　　　　out money in Iran was Kermit Roosevelt. Also Schwarzkopf's dad.

The cause of war . . . .

. . . . the locus is the leaders . . . . *

The invasion of Iraq was the conception of and inception by a determinant little power clique, in this case termed an "administration". Other times and places, "monarchy", "holy Roman Empire", "sultanate", "junta", and other names have applied. By any name, in any case, this is how the world has and still does work: the unholy ·· trinity of sheer power, religious imposition, and wealth/resource acquisition per se or through economic control of their markets. There is always an admixture of these conquest condiments, and though there may be a *focus*, (an emperor, *fuhrer* , tsar, comrade", pope, or other), such "lead man" is guided or influenced or coerced or even the outright puppet of his "intimates" and "advisors" . . . . who are generally the true representatives of the wealth and power of fief or kingdom or empire and now even hemisphere.

The immediate cast of the tragi-comedy of the present is a triumvirate of stars (Bush, Cheney, Rumsfeld), and two major supporting actors (Rice and Powell) the latter reciting and acting-out the worst bad-drama concoction of the major three.

War can be declared and simply imposed, so to speak. An empire or dictatorship has a "victim-population", the military establishment essentially an enslavement at least of the young males. From quick-death to its imposition through various durations and duress of heinously creative means (crucifixion through firing squad or life imprisonment at hard labor), populations of places and times have had no choice but to wage war for the whims of the power-elite. There can be no allowance for pacifism, etc.

But an element of war and those who fight derives from basic male human nature, it seems. Almost instinctual aggression is like an "endo-regime" so often. And some hyper-aggressive personality, thence some assemblage resulting in a quorum of intentions, and small-scale wars are almost like spontaneous aspects of psycho-social interaction. In some primitive societies, micro-warring (raids) are the *raison d'etre*.

And it is this dimension of the human that, even latent in times of peace and preoccupation with living and loving . . . . can be coerced or stirred by government and the thousands will lay down their tools and take up the offered arms and march off somehow "lemming-like" to drown in the blood of slaughter. Crusades. . the almost sportsman-like motivation to join the game of death, destruction, mutilation and disease (the plagues contracted by the few able to return home, thus to infect those at home after so doing to those along the way). Civil War.

Of course, a major factor leading to war and leading those called the warriors, is Information. Also collusion, distortion, outright lies, defamations are the components of *brainwash*. "Truth" and even "rationality", even to sophisticates and intelligentsia, can be but functions of directed propaganda or factors of media bombardment and immersion (such as what American publications and at least the Economist (English) provided us starting mid-2002 and proclaiming to us at least up to the "end" of the Iraq war.

* This, written in c 2002, as part of my
"Iraq Debacle", The "leaders" to whom it
refers could easily be recast!

Another consideration of our present situation and its ramifications is that even now when we'd assume (or have been led to believe) that compassion, conscience, and even common sense would be the right and freedom for the individual to act upon, come the orders to ship out, there's hardly a choice. As recently as the "refuseniks", prosecution and incarceration would result. Prior, dodgers were jailed and deserters shot. And a bit priorer in the land of the free, I've read that Irish immigrants essentially "impressed" into the Union army were branded on their foreheads for trying to desert the suffering and carnage.

One might assume that "in this day and age" in America, all such would be behind us in history. . . . or elsewhere from us in realms of regimes or African rampages. For our democratic system is tripartite, each checking and balancing the others. For our well-established government has, in addition, a bipart *legislative* branch elected by the people. Said branch must approve of any war in which the country will engage. And although this process obviously is not a popular-election (per se) of war-stance (for or against), it is "representative", supposedly, of the population's wishes.

There is intended implicit concensus and a comprehensive basis thereof. Ethics, opinions, beliefs, theories, even plain manias and mongerings (representing the various opinions of people) are meant to form a "data-base" by which a Presidential/military agenda and even its "intelligence" are to be evaluated.

The breadth of man's ideations distilled in the democratic institution of elected representatives' expertise and insider-involvement should . . yield the elixir of perspicacity and wisdom and thus be synergic of the "majority-merit" when a vote is taken and the checks and balances of democracy ensure truth and justice to all.

HAH !!

There are   flaws inherent in this beatifically-intended system.
We have so clearly seen them during Afghanistan and especially the Iraq debaqle.
"Redefinition" (Orwell's "newspeak"?). Exaggeration and
mere conjecture can be termed "Intelligence." Honesty
(such as about the Iraq-Africa nuclear info in the speech)
is a non-issue where "our best intelligence at the time" is the cover
or there's an underling on which to pin blame for care-
less editing or something.
The power of the Presidency and behind the government is mega-
business (military-industrial-petroleum complex). The
top politicians (administration) wear their public personas
like masks over their actual corporate faces.

Accountability and even constitutionality can simply be evaded by "executive edict" with the pseudonym of <u>National Security</u>. For example, the military can hold someone without legal aid up to , apparently, indefinitely . . . . and a military tribunal usurps the role of judicial process (court trial).

I don't think I need to continue.. This little dissertation seems sufficient as introduction to my final segment on Iraq. And certainly the material in the prior sections may adequately present a span of consideration . . . .including the veracity and validity of my editorial and philosophic promulgations . . . . . or not.

So let me simply say that I hope the following pages provide a sort of overview and review of what I've covered before. . . . . . . and maybe the images and ideas for some profound introspection about where we're at, where others are, and what such disparities may mean for our homeland security.

Big Iraq Attack!!!

. . . . looks like we found the weapons of mass destruction after all. They looted and burned and now bomb and escalate their attacks and what's next . . . . . .

The most destructive weapons are deprived and enraged people in so many nations in the world . . . .

. . . . . and now in another newly ravaged place. . . . .

Is our "War on Terrorism" but gasoline on the white-heat of rage?

MILITARY

We surely need to maintain a significant conventional armamentarium: land, air and sea things from hand-held to bombers and refuelers, tanks and trucks, and guns and gear, and floating things up to carriers carrying thousands.

We need "boots" in training and at-the-ready active.

Even slight chance of some provocation by or confrontation with China (or North Korea) is sufficient reason that we keep competently conventional.

However, 9/11 should suffice as a premise upon which to base the protocols of our preparedness!! The proportionate potentials. Hardly a chance of a foreign country coming at us with any sort of military force. Why would they waste the effort? Money? Isn't it rich? Isn't it rare? No need for ships on the sea or planes in the air. So where are the arms? There have to be explosives. They'll send in the suicidals!

The size of the US military budget, at $472 billion, is higher than that of the next 17 major nations combined and 3 times more than China. For what purpose other than defensive status? As offensive force, the offense to others has been far more pervasive in their hatred of us for invading, destroying, maiming, killing -- than any shock and awe supremacy of our prowess or the hardware of shock and awe. All the billions accomplished what, other than disruption and destruction, in Iraq? Afghanistan? And much of the world's opinion of us.

Have we become (the opposite of the "mouse that . . ") rather, "the dinosaur that roared", rattling our monster-military sabers while the viruses of extremism and terrorism (and even ecological entities) represent far more insidious and potentially invasive detriment to us -- even unto our destruction/extinction?? (A guy with a vial from regions Tigris or Nile. . . . .awaiting the right moment by . . the water supply.)

A book I obtained awhile back was titled *Killed Cartoons.* The cartoons had been submitted to, but rejected by, The New Yorker. One of them showed two stick-like figures plummeting downward beside the smoke-billowing, sketch- representation of one of the Trade Center towers. The caption read, "If only we'd had a missile defense system . . . "

Terrorism is the major threat to this and other countries (this was acknowledged by Ryan). Against terrorists, conventional weapons are the equivalent of dynamite as deterrent of cockroaches or termites. What good would Star Wars have been against the attack by in**tra**-continental ballistic missiles bearing passengers along with their fuel tanks of mass destruction??

From the British back in the 1700s to the Russians in Afghanistan to the Americans in Iraq, a fighting "force" is almost a futility of formulation and formation when confronting the dispersion of an insurgency or terrorist network even called Patriots.

An article I have mentions the Army's request to stop production of M1 tanks (42 of them for $255 million!! divides to apprx. $6,071,429 each). Despite un-need, the appropriation for their manufacture was approved. Another, the F-35 Strike Fighter ($200 million per plane) "described as 'mixed' performance" is being considered for cancellation -- but it seems the issue is not military necessity, strategic importance for our nation's strength in the eyes of its foreign beholders, even efficacy or need of the whatever . . . . but a matter of how many jobs will be lost!!! How much MIC corporate profit cancelled.

Considering "sequestration", the projection is that it "would cost more than 1 million jobs by the end of 2013 and 'The impact on industry would be devastating,' said Robert Stevens, CEO of defense giant Lockheed Martin. He told congress that his company, which received 82 percent of its revenues from the government in 2011, might be forced to furlough 10,000 of its 120,000 employees if the [D] cuts go ahead.

Here, such an interesting glimpse into the hypocrisy of R protestations against government programs being but socialistic schemes in government-subsidies'- clothing. There's been no Romney comment to the effect that we've got to bring down the deficit no matter what and if it hurts the MIC (military-industrial-complex), let market forces be and the companies succumb (a la suggestion for Detroit and banks). Above quotations and data from "The Week", October 2, 2012.

On the following pages a list of the R-proposed non-military cuts. The webside-source is noted.

Somehow, somewhat obverse to the seemingly socialistic mega-subsidy of the M.I.C. by the government (talk about "pork" -- $6+ million dollar per tank even though the army already has more almost than it has room to store)! I was saying, somehow, somewhat obverse is that these "civilian" Romney cuts almost seem to eviscerate the very organism of America as a society and culture, collaborator with its collective constituents, and colleague with other nations in some respects.

Such clear-cut harvesting of our evolved notion (and implementation) of national greatness! -- to provide for the semi-obsolete paradigm of military excess, both of material and manpower -- almost seems a treasonous attempt to subvert our *democracy*'s distribution for the fulfillment of the peoples' pursuit of happiness . . . and establish a "*militocracy*" A military nation. One nation under M.I.C.!!

Eisenhower . . hear him rolling over . . . mumbling . . . "they didn't listen . . .. "

Romney tax cuts, website source obvious on the pages following.

Hi
Thought it was worth reading
Bob

-----Original Message-----
From: etmurad <etmurad@comcast.net>
Sent: Thu, Oct 11, 2012 8:00 am
Subject: Fwd: List of Republican cuts in Ryan's plan

Subject: List of Republican cuts in Ryan's plan

List of Republican cuts. Clearly, Paul Ryan knows how to make the cuts necessary to get this country back on track.
<u>Notice S.S.. and the military are NOT on this list</u>
These are all the programs that the new Republican House has prep to the end and pass it on to as many as you can.

* Corporation for Public Broadcasting Subsidy -- $445 million annual s:
* Save America 's Treasures Program -- $25 million annual savings.
* International Fund for Ireland -- $17 million annual savings.
* Legal Services Corporation -- $420 million annual savings.
* National Endowment for the Arts -- $167.5 million annual savings.
* National Endowment for the Humanities -- $167.5 million annual savi
* Hope VI Program -- $250 million annual savings.
* Amtrak Subsidies -- $1.565 billion annual savings.
* Eliminate duplicating education programs -- H.R. 2274 (in last Congre

McKeon, eliminates 68 at a savings of $1.3 billion annually.
* U.S. Trade Development Agency -- $55 million annual savings.
* Woodrow Wilson Center Subsidy -- $20 million annual savings.
* Cut in half funding for congressional printing and binding -- $47 milli
* John C. Stennis Center Subsidy -- $430,000 annual savings.
* Community Development Fund -- $4.5 billion annual savings.
* Heritage Area Grants and Statutory Aid -- $24 million annual savings.
* Cut Federal Travel Budget in Half -- $7.5 billion annual savings
* Trim Federal Vehicle Budget by 20% -- $600 million annual savings.
* Essential Air Service -- $150 million annual savings.
* Technology Innovation Program -- $70 million annual savings.
* Manufacturing Extension Partnership (MEP) Program -- $125 million
* Department of Energy Grants to States for Weatherization -- $530 mil
* Beach Replenishment -- $95 million annual savings.
* New Starts Transit -- $2 billion annual savings.
* Exchange Programs for Alaska Natives, Native Hawaiians, and Their
Partners in Massachusetts -- $9 million annual savings
* Intercity and High Speed Rail Grants -- $2.5 billion annual savings.
* Title X Family Planning -- $318 million annual savings.
* Appalachian Regional Commission -- $76 million annual savings.
* Economic Development Administration -- $293 million annual saving
* Programs under the National and Community Services Act -- $1.15 bil
* Applied Research at Department of Energy -- $1.27 billion annual sav
* Freedom CAR and Fuel Partnership -- $200 million annual savings.
* Energy Star Program -- $52 million annual savings.
* Economic Assistance to Egypt -- $250 million annually.
* U.S. Agency for International Development -- $1.39 billion annual sav
* General Assistance to District of Columbia -- $210 million annual savi
* Subsidy for Washington Metropolitan Area Transit Authority -- $150
savings.

* Presidential Campaign Fund -- $775 million savings over ten years.
* No funding for federal office space acquisition -- $864 million annual
* End prohibitions on competitive sourcing of government services.
* Repeal the Davis-Bacon Act -- More than $1 billion annually.
* IRS Direct Deposit: Require the IRS to deposit fees for some services
processing payment plans for taxpayers) to the Treasury, instead of allov
part of its budget -- $1.8 billion savings over ten years.
* Require collection of unpaid taxes by federal employees -- $1 billion t
THE HELL IS THIS ABOUT?
* Prohibit taxpayer funded union activities by federal employees -- $1.2
ten years.
* Sell excess federal properties the government does not make use of -- !
savings.
* Eliminate death gratuity for Members of Congress.***WHAT???***
* Eliminate Mohair Subsidies -- $1 million annual savings.
* Eliminate taxpayer subsidies to the United Nations Intergovernmental
Change -- $12.5 million annual savings ***WELL ISN'T THAT SPECIAL***
* Eliminate Market Access Program -- $200 million annual savings.
* USDA Sugar Program -- $14 million annual savings.
* Subsidy to Organization for Economic Co-operation and Development
million annual savings.
* Eliminate the National Organic Certification Cost-Share Program -- $!
savings.
* Eliminate fund for Obamacare administrative costs -- $900 million sav
* Ready to Learn TV Program -- $27 million savings..***WHY?????***
* HUD Ph.D. Program.
* Deficit Reduction Check-Off Act.
* **TOTAL SAVINGS: $2.5 Trillion over Ten Years**

My question is, what is all this doing in the budget in the first place?

CIVILIAN CUTS

So these cuts would bring down the national debt . . .and "get this country back on track"? Toward a continuing recession (at least). For what would all the people dis-employed from these agencies and institutions do? Work on oil rigs? What would all those depending on the programs do? Hold up cardboard signs at street intersections because there are no more jobs on oil rigs? Or as senior citizens or disableds they couldn't get hired anywhere?

The Romney/Ryan proposal is to provide $Xtrillion in "tax relief" to restart the economy? Talk about throwing money down drains. What happened to the $X-whatever the amount was of the Bush tax breaks, proportionately highest to the most wealthy? Didn't see many jobs created! Rather, that prod to prosperity was just another push toward the plummet we're still close to the bottom of.

Tax relief. Uncut military bloatget (bloated budget). But he's going to create millions of jobs? Doing what? It would seem that unless military expenditure were increased, putting more people to work involving military manufacture or activity would not be possible without lowering wages of those now so employed, thus to share with the new influx!!

Maybe a Romney administration would issue executive order to Walmart and Apple and Gap/Old Navy and Conair and all the rest of once-America's employers . . . "This is your new President speaking. You must now return your manufacturing/assembling to your homeland and pay American wages to American workers." Or would it be, "Come on back and we'll make sure you don't have to pay your American workforce any more than you're paying your Chinese and Vietnamese and Bangladeshis and Indians and Madagascarians and South Koreans and god knows I've seen boxes (especially of clothing) with names of origin countries that I've never heard of!!! To make so much stuff that gets sold and old (and usually long before) thus ends up disposed of in such quantities that the agencies are overwhelmed and the fabric gets demoted to "rag-stock" and baled and shipped back across the seas to be made into carpet under padding and other conversion crap. (see following pages). . . . . .

There was just superficial mention of the myriad jobs Mitt will create?

Biden's reaction was like a teenager listening to the make-a-believe world-changing plans of an adolescent (which, at times, seemed Ryan's demeanor). Biden seemed amusedly disgusted, even "aghasted".

He should have demanded, "What will these jobs be? GIVE ME SPECIFICS!!!"

MEDICAL

Regarding Obamacare -- again, the stalemate of does it work and save, or not and cost. Will it benefit the populace at the expense of businesses which have to be able to pay people other aspects of "populace-benefit" (wages) -- which Obama-care costs will siphon off? Will it usurp choice? Deny services?

Ryan stated that "bureaucrats with no medical credentials" would be making decisions about medical procedures under Obama's plan. Rather a stretching, or convoluting, of the situation. This "panel" or whatever it's called, would be making decisions, but not actual medical ones. That approval of "elective" procedures might be within their domain of decision? Isn't that already the situation where insurance-o-crats make decisions concerning approval of coverage for this and that, and far from just pre-existing conditions and outright elective surgeries etc.? How many even health- (if not even life-) -involving procedures are denied coverage? And how many of those insurance company personnel have medical credentials?

A thought came to me as I heard this rather brief bit of the debate.

Having private enterprise insurance companies determining coverage, thus payment, thus often attainability of medical procedures, is not unlike foxes in charge of chicken coops. So too, sometimes, the pharmaceutical companies are predators in purportedly protective positions. Thus the need for FDA.

But regarding Obamacare, Biden stated that the AMA was in favor of the program (or most aspects of it under consideration in the debate at the moment).

Ryan didn't dispute or refute that.

ABORTION

So contentious a subject.

So contradictory the concept that the death of a mother and an unborn child (for example because of a drunken driver or a shooter), constitutes double homicide -- but the unborn "life" can be taken (within time-frame) as "maternal-domain decision" regarding her body's "reproductive rights-determination".

But that "reproductive-residency-requirement" (of at least maternal acquiescence) pervades *life*, almost as a female prerogative (as producer of life, or not). Some animal species (rabbits, for example) will "reabsorb" embryos, even fetuses, given deleterious circumstances of the environment. Some will devour their offspring, a sort of post-facto abortion from reproductive . . . into "recyclel" consumption into digestive . . . . systems!! Many other animal species, both male and female, commit consumptive infanticide.

Humans through the eons have proactively aborted and post-facto-ly "exposed" (or worse) the unborn and/or unwanted. There came to be for the born but not wanted, such "family-surrogate" institutions as work-houses, orphanages, and so much worse, such as purposely crippled beggar children kept like slaves.

The present parameters of *sanctity of life* seem to include a segment of time and cellular proliferation from conception until birth. The furor over stem cells, which would be disposed of, being used in research perhaps to heal or regenerate fully born, even adult-with-kids sufferers of diseases or dystrophies and such, seems hypocritical, or split-brained.

To preserve the sanctity of the unborn justifies killings of abortion practitioners?? Quite a distortion of "an eye for an eye" to "a sentient human being for a systemically pre-conscious cellular cluster". If the sanctity of soul exists in the just-conceived, it would follow that it exists in the ongoing-organism incarnation unto an adult person. If that adult's beliefs or actions are "sinful" (such as abortion), to commit on him (murder) what he is accused of (abortion) is but compound-crime-commission.

Even the non-violent vehement commit a sin of omission, in my estimation.

So many people with so much time to stand with their signs and their anguish that there might not be another brought into the world to, "diffusely-de facto" deprive one already alive and wracked with malnutrition, disease, and swaddled in the post-partum amnion of its own body's spews . . . while fanned by the flies..

What about the sanctity of the sentient, the sensing, THE BORN????

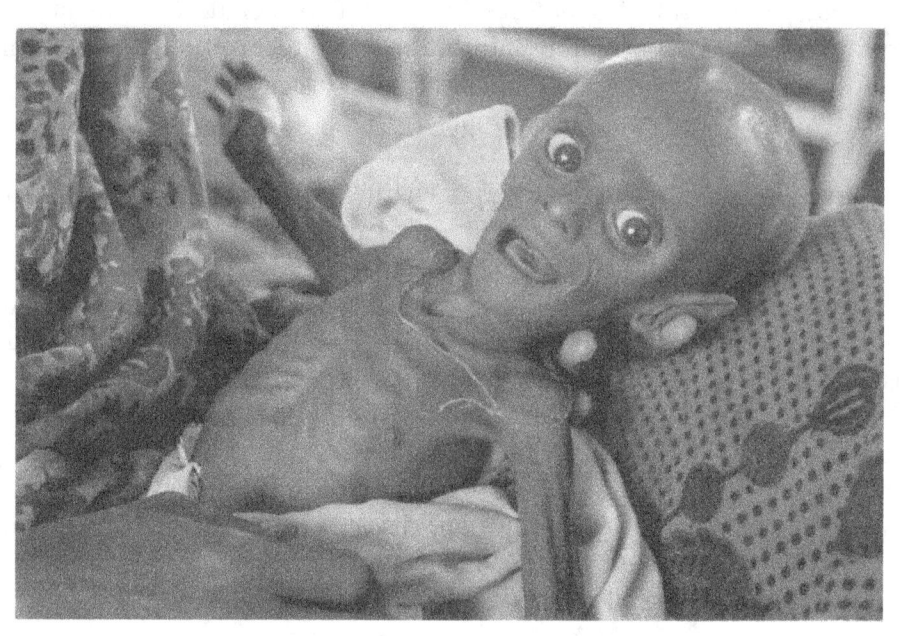

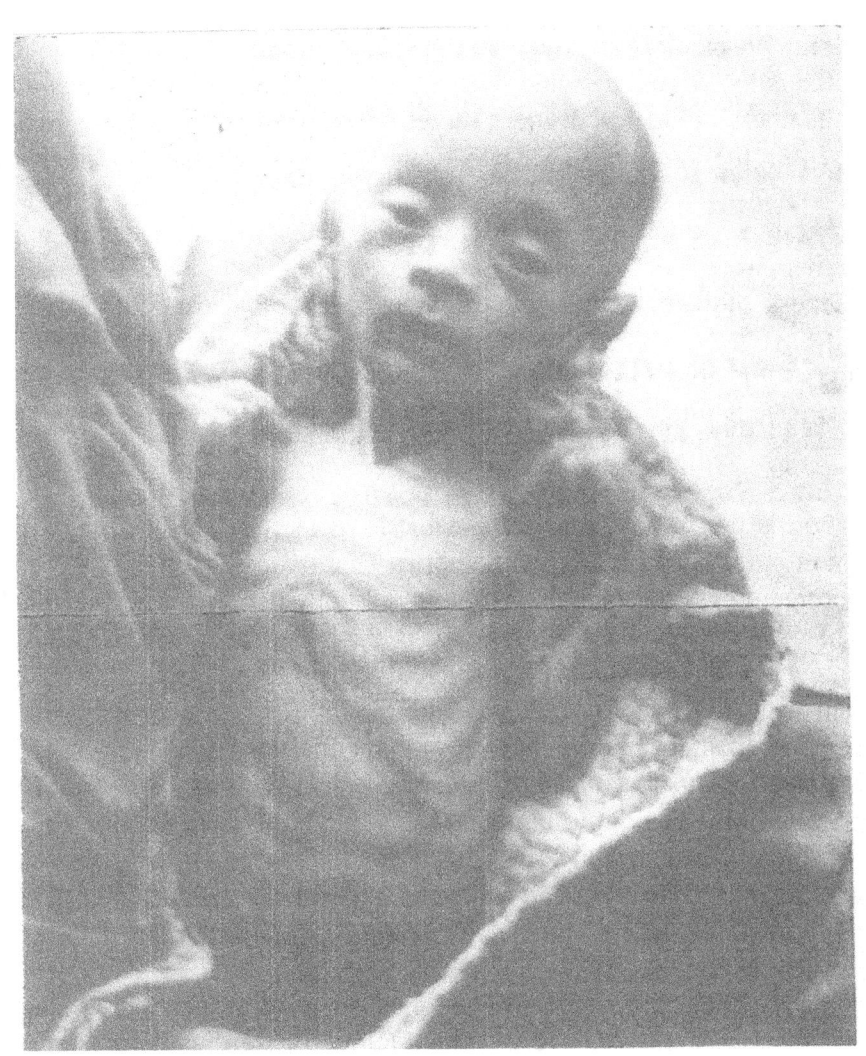

The impact of the photos above caused me to almost spontaneously sob. And there are thousands who thus suffer and waste while the "sanctity of life" is so protested and protected here by well-fed (if not fattened) self-congratulants congregated on the curb!!!.

What about the born? The starving infants?

Where are the protesters? Where are the Evangelicals? Where are the right-to-lifers when so many of the **born** so searingly suffer . . . and die . . . .slowly . . . while the signs are shaken and the voices shout and in the time they're so engaged perhaps they should, instead, be holding up pictures such as these (instead of abortion photos) and collecting money from passers-by to send to some food agency to keep the living alive -- rather than clamoring for the mass production of more sacred lives while others suffer and die.

Or live and join the thousands of AIDS-orphaned kids? What about their "sanctity of life" -- before they become psychotic killers under the auspices of The Lord's Liberation Army . . . mere training to become barbarian hordes when Alqaeda sets up shop in Africa and really gets them organized. . . . .

The sacredness of life? Rather, the self-sacrament of "caring" for that which the protesters don't have to be bothered with, especially touch. Especially those dark-skinned ones. NOMCO (not my concern). Let "free-market forces", *business,* deal with life that has already been born, hopefully ambitious enough to stand on its own two feet. The unborn can't.

If, conception is life in the same *existential status* as post-partum life, why not posit that conception is but a combination of the actual, *essential* constituents thereof -- sperm and egg. In former times, to ejaculate without a potential pregnancy receptacle thereof (woman) was held to be a sin. Onan's sin seems to have been as much *disobeying* his order to screw whomever it was, as his "spilling his seed" upon the ground. But the order to screw implied that the "seed" was the substance of life. Heaven forbid if male masturbation again becomes tantamount to "componential abortion". For how long would it take to get to *menstruation as murder* de facto? -- and all about Eve (and all females at least of some Simian species up into humans) the worst sin will be seen as this spilling of egg(s) (along with the endometrial nest??)

Pardon, I've let myself get a bit carried away.

Biden and Ryan, both acknowledged Catholics, acceded to the Church's anti-abortion stance. Both were succinct and clear. Ryan would allow for contingencies such as rape, life of mother. Otherwise Catholic doctrine would be platform, policy. Biden adhered to his Catholic faith, but excepted those with different beliefs. He did not feel that the government should impose religious conditions or constraints. The US government should not, so to speak, be the proxy of the Vatican and legislate imposition of Catholicism upon people of other faiths or non-faith, even in the area of abortion.

Thus, Biden was implying the continuation of present abortion policies and precedents (RvW), and trimester durations for termination.

To the question of Roe V. Wade that began this segment of the debate . . . perhaps Ryan should have been cornered. "Be Specific!! Would a Romney adminis-tration attempt to overturn Roe?

To the question of Roe V. Wade that began the segment . . perhaps Ryan's noticeable hesitation before responding. . . hid . . . thus revealed . . . his answer . . . . . .

CONCLUSION

Consensus represents *actuality*, an ever-fluctuating, variability. Social. Ethical. Political. Economic actuality. "Where it's at". The dynamic of the society and its component systems (government and private, social and scientific, religious and secular, etc.) is "the actuality". It's what is. Individual prejudices and predilections and philosophies and beliefs become subordinate to the eventual "composite" actuality. The process-outcome of group supersedes the individual preferences of guys and gals, straights and gays, rights-to and freedom-ofs, and all the other diversities of humankind.

This reality, "actuality", doesn't mean the individual should be subordinated, subjected without recourse. And we have established a pervasive recourse system in the "free-world" as our systemic actuality. The group as after-all determinant is a consensus, the summation of individuals (even via such computational contortions as the Electoral College). People vote. Contentions, compiled and computed, form consensus/majority which becomes formalized as "legislation" and "law". And extrapolated even from absolute antitheses of standpoints, beliefs, even expertise and perspicacity, comes the consensus spokesman.

The guy who wins the election.

Great system. It works. Even by its not working!! in that it encompasses a "governor" by means of parliamentary procedures, even those which can result in "gridlock". Better that than run-away, rampant factional impositions. Thus the protection from the extremes unto fanaticisms. Sometimes such result from consensus segments unrestrained. And the non-consenting can become victims when consensus becomes radicalized, or otherwise skewed. (Think the Sunni and Shiite shit). Think communism in China. Think Taliban.

I think we're safe from such threat. But even should a clique-consensus-surge result, say, in repealing Roe, there's that ultimate over-ride/veto/undermine/ of rule and even law and regulation -- human nature.

Back to the back alleys. Or perhaps a market for research into quite simple do-it-yourself potions soon available on the black market. The realm of drugs (drug-drugs) is a prime example of such pervasions or dispersions that law and order can't shut down.

So too was Prohibition

FINALLY TO SUMMARY

An Obama win may mean another term of only creeping recovery. For the very economic system *in toto* seems to have became a Ponzi process of making more jobs to pay more wages to provide for more purchases requiring more production requiring more wages to pay . . .(drained by such extensive off shoring of jobs).   And this "economic eddy" has been further diluted and dissipated by an incremental out-flow into the containers of billionaires and millionaires and the gold-lined cloud-chambers of the 1+ percent. Evaporation? From the vortex?

It may only have been on the basis of inflated real estate values as a "debt-collateral standard" (not a gold-standard "substantive" . . which, itself is obviously not a bedrock considering the inflation of gold/per/ounce along with other precious metals). Prosperity based on irrationally inflated real estate values, transmogrified into indebtedness (mortages), "bundled" and sold as securities (collateral debt) . . . . talk about an (at first inadvertent, but later concerted private sector) betting BLUFF!!!!!

Another consideration.

The President is represented and deprecated as a sole determinant, so to speak. The Presidency is "anthropomorphized". The President is "characterized", even as Satan (or Hitler). But he's the spokesman/"fronts-man", for the vast group of advisors and specialists which comprise the administration. Yes, in cases such as Truman's on Israel and Bush/Cheney with Iraq, determination or deviousness can divert scrutiny and screw the systemic political, legislative, bipartisan (etc.) process. But generally the government represents a kind of consensus itself.

Among Obama's advisors there are such people as Warren Buffet, hardly an incompetent regarding economics, business acumen, investment strategies, his billionaire-level far surpassing Mr. Romney's mere millions.

In spite of the idealistic and ritualistic recitation by Ryan, Mr. Romney would be facing a consensus situation not all that different from Obama. To try to implement the list of cuts (on the pages above) would bring his administration up against drastic push-back from those whose interests and dividends and wages are paid by such programs. Also by those who personally depend on the programs for survival.

Again, how many jobs would be lost by such flaying of America's fabric of societal-security . . . in order to maintain the fool-metal-jacket uniform of military superfluity?

An Obama win, -- a continuum of a significantly same scenario as the last 4 years.
A Romney regime? The direction of the political game's gridlock would just reverse. D blocking R attempts at forward-passings of platform proposals. Of late it's been the reverse. A Rommey win would probably be a case of what the rock group, "The Who", so perceptively stated as concluding lyrics of their . . . "we're marching in the streets . . . ." song.

"Here's to the new boss, same as the old boss".

The Third Debate
in brief.

Obama, as in the previous encounters, presented his administration's accomplishments, acknowledging that the economic problems have not been satisfactorily resolved, sufficient umbers of unemployed not put back to work. He noted there have been modest improvement in those areas from when he took office.

He mentioned the draw-down from Afghanistan, the withdrawal from Iraq, amending, in response to Romney's criticism, that the procedures are being carried out in collaboration and cooperation with the Joint Chiefs.

Concerning the Middle East, Iran and Syria specifically, Barack stressed that his policies are not unilateral, but represent a sort of consensus of many concerned (at least, some *contiguous* to the turmoils) nations.

Regarding Israel and Netanyahu, he denied turning his back on Israel in any way. More than once he stressed that we would stand by Israel.

In all areas, it seemed to me that Obama presented a reality, an actuality, of ongoing domestic and international dynamics. To some extent, or in some ways, either a degree of improvement, resolution, or at least removal has been accomplished or is in the process. For other matters, immediate resolution may not be possible. Especially in that those Mid-East matters are in the Middle East, for the U. S. to align itself with the interests (and possible survival) of those in the region is, itself, an accomplishment of multi-national policy. Even restraint as strength.

It seemed that Romney's presentation, as in previous appearances, was . . . promises, promises, promises. What he perceives as US weakness he'll strengthen by not letting others' interests supervene our own, our nation's prowess. For if others see us as weak we're in danger from them. He has no realization that, at least since Iraq, our "North Korea-ish" militaristic threats would be scoffed at best, beset by terrorist-backlash at worst.

His statements regarding Israel could have been read from the same policy prompter as Obama's. Israel is, of course, not only our responsibility in humanitarian dimension. Israel is our proxy military force right there in the midst of the mayhem Mid East. And Israel's protection is also the provision of votes and contributions from the significantly important (and well-off) Jewish-American-Zionist Diaspora.

Regarding military and might, Obama cited the statistic that the U.S. spends more than the next 10 nations [it's actually the next 15] put together, and three times more than China's. His position is that some of the military budget goes to redundant, unrequested, even unwanted materiel or equipment (such as tanks).

Romney's cited statistic concerned some type of naval vessel, and that we now have fewer than quite some years ago.

Barack countered that we now have far fewer horses (I think that was his example) than we used to. (The Boston Herald termed this Barack's "Snark-attack" on Romney"). Times and strategies and technologies have changed. We now have stealth jets and aircraft carriers etc. etc. He implied (if not documented) that the type of ship Mitt mentioned was, if not obsolete, unnecessary for our defense, even in modern offensive warfare's paradigm.

Again, the math. miasma: Mitt's tax relief yet debt reduction yet military-spending retention doesn't figure. Yes it does. Barack's economic policies (especially Obamacare) will bankrupt the country if not the people too. No it won't. Each had some survey or analysis to cite for corroboration.

On a couple occasions Mitt, looking almost hurt (and I wondered if this was strategize demeanor to gain sympathy) . . Mitt complained that Obama was attacking him personally. The "attacks" (rather, critiques) were on Romney's proposals, his platform -- and it seemed quite a missed opportunity that Obama didn't quite pointedly point that out.

And also, that if contesting opposing stance comprises a personal attack, then Mitt had comMitted far worse by criticizing almost everything about Barack's policies, including that he only invests in "losers" (Solyndra, Evergreen, renewables, etc.).

Mitt's proclamation of prowess was that he'd successfully and bipartisan conducted his term as governor of Mass (again, he stressed, the while, getting through a highly controversial state healthcare program not drastically different --given state-to-nation-proportions -- than Obamacare -- by "working across the isle. He also noted his accomplishments, his success, as a businessman.

Here, another missed rebuttal by Obama, I thought. In running a business one does not encounter a system of inherent checks and balances on CEO position. One may deal with some "politics" and even connivance, but "partisanship" is hardly a level of bifurcation of the operation of a corporation!!

In conclusion, Barack reiterated what has been done during his tenure.

And Mitt made more . . promises, promises . . . he's going to stimulate the economy -- going to put 15 million Americans back to work -- going cut programs that are sucking out of the economy and inflating the deficit, the first to be Obamacare -- going to get that pipeline built and make America energy independent
> and why didn't Obama, here, point out that the
> pipeline would be bringing in shale oil from
> our present biggest supplier, Canada?

. . . Mitt's going to get private enterprise back to where it feels safe to invest in American businesses and employment
> and why didn't Obama, here, point out that
> it's the government that would be (as has been)
> paying the private sector corporations that are
> involved in the making of military matters.

I heard a pervasive deprecation of a presidency that has not been able to get us out of the predicament that the proposed platform of its replacement would pursue as continuum of that of the administration prior to the present one!!!!

And you can unravel that last paragraph -- and see where it's at and where it'll be, depending on who gets elected.

Mitt,

WHAT JOBS ?

Appleton Schneider

MITT !!

You gonna put between 15 and 23 million people to work on oil drilling, coal mining, and pipe fitting? No? Of course not. But, Mitt, what other jobs. All we've heard is promises, promises. Y'er gonna put America back to work.

DOING WHAT ????
SPECIFY !!

I'll give you a few suggestions here:

How about gray-water systems for sewage and such?
For men only, how about waterless urinals by law!?
How about solar powered light through transparencies?
How wind/solar charged battery banks, making at least
　　　the lighting and light-demand (tech. devices) power
　　　a self-contained "grid" within a neighborhood, or
　　　even single building?
How about timed traffic lights to keep the traffic moving,
　　　cut fuel consumption and pollution by absurd,
　　　sometimes enraging, sequential red-lights?
How about mandating installation of after-market engine
　　　shutoffs on all cars and trucks less than, perhaps, 6
　　　years old? (Such systems are available on high-end
　　　cars now -- just touch the gas pedal and the engine
　　　is up and running instantly).
How about housing on the acres (even roofs) of office and
　　　industrial park complexes? Would sure cut commuting.
How about manufacturers' converting to repair and restore
　　　and return (or re-sell) anything from appliances to cars
　　　rather than waste so much in remanufacture -- the old,
　　　merely component-faulty thing being junked.
How about government funded (or joint venture paradigm)
　　　massive alternative energy (especially for fuel)
　　　projects? Solar, bio, Hydrogen, algal, even . . . fuel from
feces??
How about putting people to work cleaning up litter and
　　　performing other "municipal" services for pay
　　　sufficient for their health and shelter needs plus a bit
　　　more for minor luxuries -- and even pittance tax-returns
into the system?

How about a (Max.) $3,000 battery-pack powered vehicle, bare-bones equipped for safety and comfort, just for commuting?? (Might get 100mpg equivalent? No exhaust except from a mini-motor a/c or the heating.

In the following pages I'll be dealing with these ideas in more detail. The War Effort (conversion of industries and creation of jobs) for WW II got us out of the Depression. The government funded that.
Now, we need a "Peace Effort" of the same paradigm -- funded by the government to force a transformation from waste and surplus and excess and inflation that became a complex weapon of economic mass destruction.

Yeah, MITT !

Yeah, things are bad. I've recently read the number of people known to be without jobs is 20-something million. That figure includes those who, for the moment at least, have given up looking. I don't know whether "guesstimate" or "valid statistical extrapolation" added to the sum of the "known" jobless, perhaps 17 million, I've read.

Another figure I just recently read was 15 million out of work. This is a known "known" total. Fifteen million people are actively seeking employment.

Not good. And although the percentage of the unemployed has dropped from over 8 to a little less, that's still one awful lot of people without jobs.

Something's got to be done about providing jobs.

Jobs pay wages.

Without wages, people receive government assistance -- or they'd join the already homeless -- even starve. Bad enough how many have lost their homes. Worse would it be without the government providing *survival* for **its** populace. Without such "socialistic" (read, "humanitarian") emergency-intervention there would be such hardship and worse, that there would be unrest and worse. And let things come to WORST and there might no longer be the government!!

Precedents?: French Revolution. Russian . . . ..

And many more recent elsewheres around the world

There are two Presidential candidates. The economy, specifically jobs, is the primary concern of both. Get people back to work, for that will get money earned to be spent as the fuel for commerce -- thus the engine of the economy will at least run smoothly.

Maybe just as well if it doesn't again rev! It seems, ever since Reagan, the rev-olution of affluent consumerism for all was primarily running on a fuel of fumes -- credit/debt-spending. And the ascent into the atmosphere of real estate prices ("equity-affluence" assumed from inflation) was fueled by fallacious institutional investments -- and outright fraudulent private sector mortgage originators such as Countrywide (and there were myriad others even in cahoots with ratings agencies paid for Triple As).

Alas, for the while now, the economy has been significantly misfiring, though not actually stalled (as happened in the Depression when droves stood in lines for food and verily populations of men took to the roads and the rails, perhaps to find work, at least to not be another mouth to feed by staying with their families. Myriad banks and businesses closed compared to the few in this Great Recession.

We need a system, nor more of a cesstem that seemed flush, but got flushed.

Two candidates. Two "platforms".

Obama's focuses on the actual, though slow and insufficient, revival of economy during his administration. Down from over 8% unemployed. Providing government largesse-life-support to major banking institutions -- also loans for 2/3 of the auto industry, GM and Chrysler -- saved at least hundreds of thousands of jobs. (Ford was in "terminal" state too, but obtained private bailout funding, part of the collateral being the Ford logo copyright.)

The Obama administration's platform and presentation is what it's done during the last going-on four years. Things are better than they were, but not better enough. He projects that, given another term, he can keep things moving toward recovery.

The one specific "big-ticket" he proposes (not promises) is to hire 100,000 teachers.

Romney promises, promises. He's going to get America back to work. He's going to provide jobs. Stimulate the economy. Keep those tax "incentives" that Bush put in place -- in place -- so to perpetuate the amazing jump-start of the economy that they initiated . . . ??? Quite a few years since Bush's tax breaks as "Corporation catalysts" and, the while, we went into this Great Recession. Maybe I should call the tax breaks "fuses for the fireworks of hire-works" (jobs created by tax-relief incentive for business expansion). The fuse (tax breaks) was lit, oh yes.

But it seems either it wasn't connected, or the fireworks supposed to detonate were a dud -- or all in foreign countries!

But now, no matter, Romney's going to be the savior of the "Middle Class" of working America. Jobs. America back to work.

WHAT JOBS???

Perhaps he feels he doesn't need to specify. He points out that he's been a successful businessman, running companies (including running them out of existence -- and in offshore locations), thus has the experience and qualifications and credentials to properly handle the *business* of the government. (But at the same time his stance is that the government has no business being the bailout or even benefactor of business!!) -- except, it seems, via subsidies to the mega-sector such as Agriculture, Petroleum, and outright blatant paying for the whole Military-Industrial Complex.

But, again, other than those paid for by the government, WHAT JOBS??

The number of government-funded programs he intends to cut will put a sizeable number of people out of those jobs -- thus adding to the ones who'll need jobs!

Romney proposes to drill for oil. Offshore. Onshore including wilderness and wildlife preserves. Federal land, Private land. More oil drilling. More domestic production (thus depletion of) our energy reserves.

But increase of Jobs!!!

But how many of the unemployed millions can be hired for (or be able to work on) oil rigs or platforms? I'm only guessing here, but let's say an oil platform involves 500 jobs: those actually on and running the thing, others servicing it, providing supplies of various kinds from hardware to food, and transportation workers.

So per platform or land-based facility we have 500 people put back to work. To get 500,000 people off the "47%er dole" we'll need 1,000 oil drilling facilities!!

Well, if we go with the 15 million unemployed figure (from my earlier page), that leaves 14 million five hundred thousand people still looking for jobs that Mitt's so enthusiastically and animatedly promising to provide.

"Clean coal"! He specified that too in the debate. How long will that last now that we're, so to speak, performing mountain mastectomies to get it, rather than "linear lumpectomies", the former procedures of actually mining?

And, coal, oil, or other, wouldn't it be wiser to keep what we got just in case our great grand children might need it? Like the petro and natural gas, we know it's there and we have proven technologies to extract, transport, convert to fuel these **resources**. Some of which will always be needed such as for major industrial processes, motors, etc. even if alternative energy systems become viable.

But what if alternatives don't work out . . . . ? The preserved conventional resources would have to become "alternatively productive" by the hyper-efficiency of future engines, generators, heating, etc. (Or society would have to revert to a former way of life!!)

Mitt considers natural resources to be commodities, mere products, their immediate primary value in putting people to work to make money -- but also to make profits for business!!

Good luck pumping more petro and gas prices going back down to where they once were. What need? People are in rampant mobility even with the present prices.

And wouldn't it be far better to continue increasing fuel efficiency, thus decreasing fuel consumption (requiring more drilling)? If you're getting 30% more mpg, prices can go up 30% and you're even!! If you're driving back and forth to work in a "commuta-car" (one of my listed suggestions at the beginning of this writing) . . and you're getting the equivalent of 100 mpg, $6 per gallon gas would still leave you saving money from what you're spending now to drive that $20,000+ combination space-ship and yacht through the traffic, maybe achieving (given the stop-and-start) well less than 10 mpg?

Jobs. Mitt-jobs.

WHAT JOBS ??
He hasn't specified or listed or enumerated or suggested.
Except . . . .

He'll get that pipeline built!!!
That's the pipeline from Canada which, it seems is being blocked because it's routed over a major American aquifer. There's proven possibility of catastrophic spillage (BP, Caribbean -- prior, Exxon Valdez -- and in between, many little pipe leaks). In view of even the slight percentile (distance of pipeline over aquifer/overall length of pipeline), to chance petro-pollution of precious (and diminishing) water . . . is not just unconscionable but, from a broad business perspective, reckless. (From an environmental standpoint, criminal!!)
But that pipeline he's going to get built because it will provide jobs. Of the fourteen million three hundred thousand people **not** back to work (500,000 drilling oil + I'm proposing an arbitrary 200,000 involved with that "clean coal" = 14,300,000 still unemployed) . . . how many of them would become pipe-fitters and fill the associated and ancillary and support positions to bring in the Canadian oil?
If it's so important to build the pipeline, just what's the problem with re-routing it? A little lengthier? Maybe that'll require a few more jobs!! More people back to work.

More imported energy. From Canada. Already our major "foreign" source. (What happened to that "American energy independence" bit, Mitt? Maybe you're heavily invested in Canadian shale?)
OPEC provides a smaller percentage to the multi-national petro-"Pool" (other suppliers being Mexico, So. American countries including Venezuela, Norway, etc. etc. see list that follows here.)
Now add more domestic production too, what with all the U. S. drilling on- and off-shore Romney proposes. There would be a lot more of petro-products (gas and diesel etc.) on the market. Maybe prices would come down some?
If so, consumption would increase, no doubt, as people would just drive more and more. And there'd be less concern about shutting off lights

what with lower electric bills. Conservation? For what?? It's cheap again!!! USE IT UP!!!! We've put so many people back to work drilling and trucking and in the tourism business etc. They're making money to go out and buy more stuff too, so much of it made in part from petroleum. Let's use it up!!

It's ours!! Our energy "independence" in Mitt's short-sighted perspective!! American oil production increased. GET IT OUT!! USE IT UP!! Same with coal. Natural gas. The latter seems to be potentially the biggest energy reserve. Vast pockets of natural gas to be tapped -- one projection being 200 years'-worth at present usage.

That's enough for a little over 2 generations hence!!

Domestic petroleum reserves? Seems there's not as much as gas.

Coal? Probably even less.

"Conventional energy sources" are FINITE resources. Depleted, they're depleted. Gone, they're gone. Their chemical/molecular formulation took millions of years.

But the one party's platform proposes to pump and mine and frack and lower price to increase consumption . . . . . talk about self-centered, short-term, stupidity!!

Political idiocy because it panders to pathology in "patriotism's" embodyment!!!

Even if Mitt's paradigm of productivity were sufficient to put population-equivalent numbers of people back into jobs!!

Crude Oil and Total Petroleum Imports Top 15 Countries

September 2011 Import Highlights: Released November 29, 2011
Monthly data on the origins of crude oil imports in September 2011 has been released and it shows that three countries exported more than 1,000 thousand barrels per day to the United States (see table below). The top five exporting countries accounted for 69 percent of United States crude oil imports in September while the top ten sources accounted for approximately 88 percent of all U.S. crude oil imports. The top five sources of US crude oil imports for September were Canada (2,324 thousand barrels per day), Saudi Arabia (1,465 thousand barrels per day), Mexico (1,099 thousand barrels per day), Venezuela (759 thousand barrels per day) and Nigeria (529 thousand barrels per day). The rest of the top ten sources, in order, were Colombia (510 thousand barrels per day), Iraq (403 thousand barrels per day), Ecuador (299 thousand barrels per day), Angola (283 thousand barrels per day) and Russia (275 thousand barrels per day). Total crude oil imports averaged 9,006 thousand barrels per day in September, which is a decrease of (16) thousand barrels per day from August 2011.

Canada remained the largest exporter of total petroleum in September, exporting 2,829 thousand barrels per day to the United States, which is an increase from last month (2,637 thousand barrels per day). The second largest exporter of total petroleum was Saudi Arabia with 1,479 thousand barrels per day.

Crude Oil Imports (Top 15 Countries)
(Thousand Barrels per Day)

Country	Sep-11	Aug-11	YTD 2011	Sep-10	YTD 2010
CANADA	2,324	2,240	2,157	1,937	1,971
SAUDI ARABIA	1,465	1,075	1,180	1,082	1,072
MEXICO	1,099	1,150	1,113	1,108	1,132
VENEZUELA	759	806	893	919	928
NIGERIA	529	854	826	1,107	1,018
COLOMBIA	510	365	364	308	328
IRAQ	403	637	473	422	464
ECUADOR	299	303	203	229	215
ANGOLA	283	311	323	404	413
RUSSIA	275	252	246	286	295
BRAZIL	163	213	225	177	270
KUWAIT	145	165	164	172	204
ALGERIA	139	140	204	366	337
CHAD	74	32	54	30	14
OMAN	72	52	39	0	0

Total Imports of Petroleum (Top 15 Countries)
(Thousand Barrels per Day)

Country	Sep-11	Aug-11	YTD 2011	Sep-10	YTD 2010
CANADA	2,829	2,637	2,670	2,479	2,537
SAUDI ARABIA	1,479	1,075	1,187	1,093	1,086
MEXICO	1,192	1,185	1,218	1,254	1,260
VENEZUELA	806	906	979	1,008	1,007
RUSSIA	592	585	609	648	624
NIGERIA	580	892	876	1,174	1,053
COLOMBIA	529	395	395	363	360
IRAQ	404	637	473	422	464
ECUADOR	305	309	205	229	217
ANGOLA	304	331	335	417	422
ALGERIA	291	298	396	543	512
VIRGIN ISLANDS	189	185	189	302	261
BRAZIL	188	228	240	181	289
ARUBA	149	81	79	0	0
KUWAIT	145	165	165	172	206

Note: The data in the tables above exclude oil imports into the U.S. territories.

Eh, why should Romney, as representation of ethics and ethos of his echelon (and party), give a damned about so distant a future as that of his childrens' children's children or even sooner? There's so much money to be made now if people are back to production, making money to go into the Corporate coffers via their consumption.

But there's another argument for "drill America" (bringing to mind a "shaft" -- also regarding exploiting conventional coal mining).

This second delusion (the first that the unemployment crisis will be solved) is that by becoming "energy-independent", America will be more secure.

First, terminating our consumption of foreign energies would mean our independence, yes . . . for the while we so greatly increased the exploitation and depletion of our own domestic reserves.

But, second, revenue to foreign sources of petroleum at least provides for their regimes, even if but little benefits their people. But it would be the "regimes" that would recruit from the rank and file the insurgents and terrorists, or establish actual militias or military -- and become "operant enemy states" vs. America -- if we shut them off -- and thus they'd have nothing to lose.

Third, from here and there, even including Venezuela (and its dear leader Chavez), we have been *getting* petro. We can even include OPEC in this present paragraph's context of international status, potential threat, of "foreign oil" suppliers. What actual, functional, threat do these countries present to the U. S. other than possibly increasing their prices or nationalizing some drill-rig or refinery or something? And if they got too pushy, there's always the Iranian paradigm to pursue -- have the CIA overthrow their government. Same scenario, since, in Indonesia (Aceh). These "foreign oil" sources are really at the mercy of the all but omnipotent petroleum corporations, ExxonMobil the epitome. Shit happen? Exxon exits. What's it care about one mere trickle-in of global petroleum (or gas) sources?

Fourth, China and even Russia are greater threats to US *supremacy* (economic), hardly at all to national *sovereignty* (unless something brings about military confrontation). Our natural resource (and other) trade (globalism) with them is a form of détente. Not being enemies is beneficial for both sides -- if it's profitable. Terminate that mutually assured economic mutualism (or at least symbiosis) and he thinks we'd be safer ??

Another perspective on the global petro sources: say we shut off buying petro from Bmwarbambia in Africa or SanPetdrotonia in So. America in order to be "energy independent"? They'd just sell to the eager buyers of China and Russia (and others). That would be enhancing our security -- in any way at all??

So far I've discussed what does not solve our present problems.

So far I've indicated that more conventional energy extraction and consumption would result in far more serious future problems.

HOW INDEPENDENT OF FOREIGN ENERGY SOURCES WILL AMERICA BE WHEN IT USES UP ITS OWN RESERVES??

So far I think I've made it obvious that pumping and piping oil and exploiting coal will still leave millions without jobs.

As for the military, Mitt says "no cuts", but doesn't promote increases -- so that won't provide more M.I.C. jobs.

My concern in this writing is that neither of the candidates (nor anyone else) *seems to get it.*

The **"it"** is that the very economic system is faulty, fallacious, failed. It's premise is a monetary-perpetual-motion-machine. It's outcome is a Ponzi paradigm, exacerbated by expectation of ever-increasing GDP -- but evaporating monetary circulation into profits converted into dividends and immense remunerations which retain "money" as "wealth" for the rich. From whence it doesn't "trickle-down" sufficiently. Obviously of late. Not even a trickle into jobs. Seems like Mitt realizes Obama's "trickle-down government" isn't sufficient. It's going to require Mitt's massive, big-time, big-monetary immersion in government-provided jobs (such as petro-chem. and MIC.) Yes, government-funded, the billions involved.

Nobody seems to get . . . IT . .

The crux of the "it" is WHAT KIND OF JOBS otherwise, Mitt? Your mining and pumping and piping won't put the nation back to work.

Aspects of the "it" that they don't get.

The first (1) of the "subset considerations" of the multiphase "it".

Communism didn't work. Doesn't work. Won't work. From the catastrophic failures (and atrocities) involved in Russia and China and elsewhere we have ample evidence. From the micro-membership experiments in "utopian" sects and societies in the U. S. we've seen the fallacy and failure too.

Socialism per se doesn't work. Much the same reason that Communism doesn't. Human <u>nature</u> is an infrastructural absolute, so to speak. Man's basic nature is competitive (his cooperative unto altruistic endeavors and acts usually depending on his having attained security (if not supremacy) first. Financial supremacy yields philanthropy, for example.

Man's basic nature requires something for his efforts: recognition, respect, remuneration, *reward* in the form of monetary and/or material possession. Take away the arena, the incentive, the goals . . for inspiration, intention, contention, competition, even greed and materialistic or managerial megalomania . . . and things just slump to the least productive as the level of aspiration because that's the *easiest* (keeping <u>down</u> with the Joneskys on the commune). No system for upward mobility? No system for upward mobility!! *Competition*-to-reward for achievement is the dynamic of viable socio-economic system.

Capitalism is Darwinian.

Capitalism is based on ambition, incentive competition.

Capitalism is a dynamic beyond survival of the fittest in that the less than fittest so much survive quite adequately (The Dollar Stores vs. Niemen Marcus, for one off-the-wall extreme example).

Capitalism results in extinction (or obsolescence) of the *very unfit* (or come-to-be outdated due to innovation).

Capitalism is a "binary" system. Management and labor. Their separation as adversaries, rather than components of a requisite *single* process, is fallacious, myopic. Without the labor force, what possible value, let alone "worth", would the managerial levels represent? But without management, labor would be a peasantry unless from its ranks a managerial and organizational echelon emerged.

It takes both "sides". There have been swings of exploitation. Way back almost cruel exploitation of workers by robber-barons and their manager-minions. Conditions in mines and mills, garment districts and slaughter-houses have been documented to our horror. There have come to be reciprocal effects of labor demands and management concessions actually resulting in driving enterprises out of business (such as a lot of trucking companies that could no longer afford union wages and benefits -- and obviously, of late, almost the whole automotive industry). American wage-levels and union-won benefits resulted in the "exploitation of management". This resulted in driving enterprises out of the country to foreign places where dirt-cheap wages represented survival income to people no longer able to all survive as peasants. Of course greater corporate profits (not just the corporation's survival) factored into the off shoring too.

Capitalism's give and take (or labor-management reciprocities of take and take) are part of the system.

But, *laissez faire*, uncontrolled (for such market forces do become uncontrollable -- like warfare) . . . "dog-eat-dog" dynamics not only defeat the least fit. Through the deluded daring of the Alpha level ascension of the "market" (such as investment banks). . . . the whole system has come close to collapse -- had it not been for Federal money to keep the private sector from domino-implosion.

We may have very high unemployment, but we're surely not in a 2nd Depression

But we have a huge number of people out of work.

And we've heard what almost seems platform hypocrisy -- Mitt so much condemning Osama's "trickle-down government", but Mitt's promise to put America back to work . . . which he, even in his multi-millionaire, industrialist-investor expertise, has contributed nothing toward . . . . . but will accomplish only when he's the head of the government!!!

Government leases lands and waters for drilling. Cheap. Government pays the military budget, thus provides federal funding of military industrial complex in all its complexity.

But, as I think is obvious (without my having pointed it out above), any increasing employment in these areas will only be a trickle-out from the unemployment lines.

WHAT OTHER JOBS, MITT?

There was the Depression.

Banks failed, one after the other.

Businesses closed.

The economy went into "collateral arrest" or something like that.

Now let's consider this dire scenario and say that any remedy or renaissance of the country rested solely on what the private sector would do. Even if the fortunes of the fortunate were provided as "seed money" to re-start manufacturing and commerce, and also provide mortgage relief to keep farmers on land and people in homes . . . . even with the contribution of all their millions, the millionaires could not have provided enough to prime the pump of the populace's prosperity!!

IT TOOK THE GOVERNMENT.

It wasn't a socialistic insurgency or conspiracy.

It was economic salvation from the curse of uncontrolled Capitalism's free-market mania-become massacre!!.

No, there was not a Saint Roosevelt. There wasn't even a Savior

Roosevelt. His radio chats were great public relations, personalizing the Presidency for the people. But his programs putting people back to work building walls and taking photographs and repairing roads and all (WPA the best known of them) hardly would have been sufficient to put the whole nation back to work and into an economic system. (We have here a precedent for perceiving the present percentage of re-employment only through Mitt's recovery programs).

How many walls could be built? Roads repaired? Pictures taken? Paintings painted? Etc? Even with the larger projects such as Blue Ridge Highway, proportionately few were put back to work. Other massive public works projects such as the Hoover Dam helped but a small segment of the destitute populace.

To get things moving out of the Great Depression IT TOOK THE GOVERNMENT'S most massive ENTERPRISE . . . . . THE WAR EFFORT!!

No, the government itself didn't set up shop to make tanks and guns and ammunition and aircraft and all in converted halls of congress or even the Pentagon.

The government massively funded private enterprises to convert from peacetime manufacture to wartime production. And with government funding, these enterprises re-employed the thousands and thousands who were not taken into the military itself. The female-workforce, the "Rosie the riveters" (and all the other military manufacture capacities of employment) were earning their wages **from the government** (which paid for the war-effort conversions and costs of the private sector companies). Those companies wrote the pay checks, yes. But they were paying-out what the federal government had paid-in!

That was then. There was a war going on already. There isn't now. In the paradigm of "conventional warfare" we could get involved back then. Perhaps we should have before. But the "theaters" of the war were far from our shores -- separated from Germany and Japan by oceans.

Now, what's a mere ocean? ICBMs are probably not as much of a worry as would be individuals with suicidal synergy to whatever weaponry or viral-ry they might be carrying on an inbound commercial flight.

No, the present world is no place to start a war to provide jobs.

Any massive military buildup would not only be counter-productive from the standpoint of "threatening" -- thus switching that "détente-mutualism" of trade competition (China) to an "arms-race". And in the present paradigm of threats to any nation, spending billions on massive conventional weaponry would be spending billions on obsolescence!! We have to maintain advanced and sufficient conventional armed forces (land, sea, air, and on foot). But "maintain" may be the pertinent term here. Billions for higher-tech etc. may be no more effective in our "strength" vs. aggressor threat -- than billions for exploring moon or mars would be for our "survival" in case of approaching meteor.

The economy is not going to be resuscitated by the government's conversion to militaristic manufacturing of the auto industries or appliance manufacturers or any other major employers from whom people have been laid off.

So far I've noted that drilling and mining and military and even neo-militarism won't put the country back to work.
SO WHAT JOBS WILL ??

The jobs created by the new effort to defeat the enemy -- unemployment!!
WE MUST MOBILIZE A
PEACE EFFORT

The government must provide the economic "surge" to start us on the road to an economic victory -- an economic and employment revitilization through innovations.

And not just the "conventional 'alternatives' (wind, solar, etc.)" .

Why not just put people back to work doing what they were doing before, if government is going to provide the "mobilization" funding?

For one reason (1), because we shouldn't use resources for and what we don't really need more of -- and are running out of room to dispose of. This surplus and excess of stuff so much comprises "retail". And (2) most of that manufacture actually takes place in other countries, much to the advantage of major US corporations such as Walmart, electronics, toys, trinkets, and you-name-it, because of cheap wages -- and the "false-advantage" to the American consumers of cheap prices . . . . has, in part, cost our domestic economy its jobs!

But I imagine, if cornered, Mitt would advocate bringing more and more of those jobs making more and more of that plastic stuff (and all the rest that everyone's got to get, then tries to get rid of at the yard sale. Consumer goods for consumer consumption, the more the bigger the job base and bottom line.

How, pray tell, would the off-shored jobs be brought back to our shores? Tariffs to force those corporations to bring home their employees? No chance, for that would force American retail to raise prices in order to pay American workers. For if they were able to maintain labor costs equivalent to abroad, the American workers (1) wouldn't work for pittance, and (2) if they did, wouldn't earn enough to have sufficient disposable income to be proportionate consumers for the products they'd be producing here!!!!

Global labor is here to stay. Rather, much of it is "there to stay".

But what about here?

The mobilization of the new "war-effort" here? The "Peace-effort".

What would be the areas of employment in the realm of "unconventional 'alternatives' "?

At this point I'll stop analysis and dissertation.

At this point it's ideas not just to put people back in jobs and earning money. The ideas I'm going to present would save money and save resources, all the while providing nationwide (and beyond) opportunities for the private sector whose enterprises would be the actual employers, manufacturers, installers.

Like the WW II mobilization effort, the present Peace Mobilization Effort though the manufacturing transitions, retooling, revisions and such . . . and the capital "surge" to get new systems of systems (and such) instated . . . *would come from the Federal Government.*

Call it socialistic. Go ahead. Socialistic it would be in the same way as government subsidies to agriculture and technology and pharmaceuticals and airlines and railroads and rapid transit systems and schools and public service employment and interstate highways and much more. There would be three differences: almost a majority of the categories I just mentioned required subsidies in order to stay in business.

My ideas (1) would not be ongoing life-support systems (such as farm subsidies or "federalization" of railroads and airlines etc. They'd be enhancements of our ways of life and systems of living. And (2) the R&D and manufacture and installation and implementation of these "neo-mobilization" (I'll call them) efforts would provide capitalistic returns, profits, to the private enterprises involved. Thus economic-system flow: wages, spending, tax bases, profits, dividends, a flow between the multi-level reservoir levels of the economy. Finally (3) These ideas and products and systems would save a fortune in conventional energy costs.

Best I get to the ideas. The innovations. The systems-inventions.

Quite a few are already in existence. But there needs to be the incentive of government funding to enterprises to hire and manufacture and install such new devices and systems on a "mobilization" scale. And also to assist consumers in costs to purchase such things . . . . .

Such as things that let *direct sunlight* be the source of solar powered lighting!!

One such device is called a "skylight". They come in all sizes and shapes and various materials. They're already manufactured and distributed, but used rather sparingly. One here and there on houses. And on those vast expanses of flat warehouse or big-box store roofs there may be a few. Seen from below, within the commercial buildings, except on exceptionally cloudy days, enough light comes from the rare skylight that it pretty well matches the illumination from an electricity-powered fluorescent fixture. Were there as many skylights as there usually are light fixtures, there'd hardly be need for electricity for lighting during the day.

To retrofit roofs with skylights would put a whole lot of people to work in established skylight-making industry, and contractors on roofs cutting rectilinear holes and installing them. And think of the electricity that would be saved.

To roof anything, is it really necessary to block out the sun and sky? Surely with the miracles of plastics and carbon fiber and other interfaced technology, transparent roofing could be developed. Sunny day, open louvers and let the (yes, fusion-reaction solar powered) light flood into the warehouse or store or even office, school, whatever.

So many people would go to work in the new industry of see-through roofing. And there'd be a lot making the louver devices to control just how much light (and with it heat) would come on down.

In other situations, a product (one called Solatube) is like an 8" or bigger duct, but highly reflective inside so that the light entering from above is "bounced" even thru bends and fittings to emerge, almost bulb-bright, inside the structure. (Think fiber-optic cable writ very large).

This system of "ducting light" should be mass marketed and even mandated, to let the sun take the place of the coal-fired (or even Nat'l gas) generating plant. And so many jobs would be created making the tubes, transporting, installing. With more R&D it might be possible to duct sunlight even into lower floors of high-rises. One way would be with enhanced reflectivity ducts all the way from top down. An alternative would be to have "collectors" (think a kind of satellite-dish setup) on sun-side of building, supplying even just the floor it's on the wall of.

But of course we should continue producing solar panels to convert sunlight into electricity, not just surrogate electric lighting. I see more and more panels in my travels.

With separate circuitry just for lighting or techno re-charging, etc., and for the illumination of L. E. Ds, it seems one could have a small bank of panels on the roof to provide total power, either directly to fixtures, or via a battery bank to store charge for times of dark or insufefficient sunlight. (Aside from acres-spreads of solar panels only here or there, I see single panels atop or beside innumerable highway signals and signs, temporary for construction sites, and permanent as well.

Had the government provided farm-type subsidy to Solectra or Solyndra or those other Obama "fool's investments in boondoggles" . . . a lot of people would be at work making and installing the solar systems that surely seem to be at least viable "collaborating alternatives" with (though not total replacements of generator plant electricity.

Solar and wind generation of DC current (thereby allowing storage), would also entail constructing and wiring "centralized grids" to provide electricity for the "light-uses" of illumination and tech. A bank of panels or roof-top turbine (preferably both as a "binary" system, might make each building, even house, a self-powered

unit (except for the electric stove, heat, or air conditioning.
Those would circuit from the conventional grid.
The setup would be somewhat like where someone has
a stand-by generator in case of power-outage. Only rather
than a single circuitry for everything in the house (or other
building), the conventional grid would feed a high demand
circuit: stove, heat, a.c.. The rest of the wiring could stay
as is, but connected to the "alternative" power source (s).

In a world of increasing population but decreasing water
resources (due, in part to global-warming/de-glaciation thus decrease in
river-flow volume . . . that purer water than most of that population has to
drink is used for by the advanced nations for shit and piss . . . . . is
unconscionable. Criminal!!!
All urinals should be waterless by law. Already they're being
installed in various places such as highway rest areas. They should be
everywhere. Look at all the jobs making them and replacing the flush-
ones.
There might come to be a lot of jobs reprocessing the ceramic
material of the removed ones into some kind of aggregate.
Toilets per se should use only "grey water" -- that which has
been collected from the rain on the roof . . and, as well, from the sinks
(and in residential realms, even from the washing machine and
dishwasher).
This would entail dual-system plumbing. Wastewater would be
stored in a tank which would feed to the toilets. Pure water would come
from the faucets, yes. That used would drain into the "gray-water"
cistern.
Think of the jobs that innovation of preservation of our most
precious resource (water) would create!! Think the precedent -- back in
the late 1800s when plumbing itself was introduced and had to be
installed from scratch in buildings of all kinds.
The same massive conversion, of course, installed gas-lighting
systems, then replaced them with wiring for electrical. All from scratch!!

So obviously it could be done with innovative new systems such as I'm considering here.

Sewage. Rather than just gather it and treat it, why not convert this universally available resource into energy? With the right "digestion" process, shit yields methane. Though a worse greenhouse gas than CO_2 methane can be used to power combustion engines (or be burned to produce steam for turbines).

Doubtful that there'll ever come a revision of toilet-tech so that one's bolus goes into a container to be collected for the energy digester -- rather than goes kersplush into a bowl of water to be flushed. But from the confluence of the sewer pipes and regional pumps, the resource, now just "treated" at existing facilities, could be converted. The whole system is already installed and in operation in almost all the world's urban areas. All that would be required for shit-to-energy production would be the final processing.

Think of the jobs manufacturing sewage digesters!!

There's no chance people are going to give up their conventional automobiles with all those bells and whistles and automatic features including almost self-parking now, I believe.

But to go back and forth through stop and start (or at least creeping) rush hour traffic in such costly luxury? Does it make sense, considering the thing has an engine that can make it go 65 mph (legally -- much faster actually), and thus a factor of its fuel *inefficiency* in traffic jams is costing the driver, and the environment?

How about fully enclosed golf-cart type "commuta-car", electric motor run off the kind of batteries that are used in fork lifts or pallet jacks (thus readily on the market). A few safety features, perhaps a propane heating device, radio, . . . who needs much more to go the 30 or so miles to and then back from where the thing is parked all day (and all night).

Think of all the jobs making the "commuta-cars". Think of the extent to which the components are already on the market -- as golf carts, material-handling-equipment batteries, etc.

Priced right, think how many people would spend in order to save perhaps more than the thing would cost as the alternative to the conventional car for commuting.

For weekends, vacations, other trips, one would still utilize the luxury and technology of the Toyota or Lexus or Ford or whatever.

But for those who would still use the car-car to and from and within the city (this would include cabs and delivery vehicles, etc.) there should be the after-market shut-down systems mandated. Come to a stop over X number of seconds and the engine shuts off. Touch the gas pedal and instantly it resumes internal combustion operation. (Obviously this instant off and on exists in electric and hybrid systems).

That hundreds of vehicles stopped in traffic have their 4, 5, 6, or 8 cylinders all firing away turning gasoline or diesel into carbon atmospherics is criminal.

The hundreds (probably thousands) of people who could be put to work manufacturing and installing idle-shutoff systems would be blessing to the economy.

Where there are frequent traffic lights, there should be sensor systems (or timing) so that when the red you're at turns green, the light you approach turns green, and the next, and the next. Years and years ago in New York City this timing seemed to be the case along the major avenues. Start at one light, maintain speed, and you could make it through numerous ones, turning green for your approach.

So often I now drive through sections where every one of 4 or 5 lights will turn red just as I get to it -- at the prescribed speed limit. With the technology available that's insane as well as wasteful of fuel and polluting of the air (and likely damaging of the drivers' emotional stabilities).

If so many of those roadside temporary and permanent signs are powered by a single solar panel, it would seem that almost all lights could be. Those that are already wired could be circuited to be powered only by the solar panel as long as there would be sufficient sunlight to keep the battery-pack charged. Otherwise the wiring would provide power.

Think of the jobs.

In numerous cases as I drive in the dark, I notice that the illumination from reflective surfaces (signs, markers, reflectors per se,) along the roads and intersections -- is brighter than that from the electric lights. Some of the latter are almost sky-high on the interstates exchanges.

Also, factor in the intensity of headlights now.

And consider that if there's no one on the road at a point there's really no need for lighting at all!!

So why all that electricity burned all night long? Even if it's from solar power??

Perhaps some innovative expansion of reflectivity as actual illumination (not just delineation) would be functional -- and provide jobs -- and income not only to the workers but companies involved.

That people embark on their mini-migrations from home to work and back every day results from what we defined as progress. Progress was to live in suburbia, an hour's drive away from work. Two hours (at least) taken up away from the time one could be home with family or activities otherwise. Time sitting in the luxury of the consuming and fuming highway-paradigm vehicle (again, some surely seem the fusion of space-ship and yacht). Costing $50, $60, a week for the gas. Then the parking in the city. The depreciation.

That adds up to a lot of money spent to creep along and be frustrated by "rush" hour sclerotic clotting (the traffic and one's own cardio-vascular damage?).

More and more should be able to "tele-commute". If one can sit in a cubicle with a computer in an office building, should one not be able to function just as well in an office with a computer in his home?

But in how many cases could office buildings be converted to contain housing? High-rise-with-a-view housing for those who work on the commercial floors of the building? The utilities systems are already installed but for "branches" to apartments' kitchens or bathrooms.

On the roof could be combination park/playground, solar collection, maybe garden plot. On the residential floors there could be public areas for exercise or other recreation.

Up in the morning, breakfast, dress, and walk to the elevator.

Think of the money and resources saved. Think of the pollution abated.

Think of the jobs creating the "mixed-use" conversions.

And out in the suburbs there are those vast campuses of "garden-apartment-format" office and industrial parks. So much land. Why not build condo-housing on some of the lawns? Why not on those acres of flat roofs?

The employment domain becomes the residential as well. Up in the morning, off on foot across the walkway -- or down from the rooftop housing.

Think of the time saved for living, rather than commuting!!

Think of the money saved. The petro saved. Thus the de facto vast reduction in gasoline costs (because, not commuting, one wouldn't be using much of any!!!)

Think of all the jobs building the condos.

But concerning traveling the highways.

So many (almost daily) the times.

Traffic is moving along at 65, well-spaced, could well be spaced into two of the three lanes without crowding. But the three lanes of scattered cars race along until they come upon where cars from another road merge. Now, last minute, and with yet another lane's worth of cars (these bumper-to-bumper), the three lanes have to squeeze into two.

And everything comes to a start-stop, creep, cut-in clog for fifteen or twenty minutes.

Think how many jobs could be created by instituting a system of lane-shift far ahead of the merge. The two lanes thus meshed together without slowing would continue to race along while the merging traffic would have its own "entry-lane" (the right, vacated one) in which to achieve highway speed, themselves, mesh into the other lanes -- or stay put in the right!

Maybe electrical signaling would be the way. "All traffic begin merge into left two lanes unless exiting highway at the next interchange".

An alternative, more expensive, would be to actually create a couple miles' length extra access lane from the merge. And in a couple cases I frequently traverse, there are two lanes of merge that clog into the three lanes of highway. At the very least, the merge traffic should be funneled down to one lane before joining the highway.

Traditional cloverleaf configurations were designed for much lighter traffic. Gridlock of swirls seems to be the situation at the height of rush hour. Traffic exiting one highway has to merge with that of the highway being entered, that lane of which is trying to exit. And this becomes a four-way fallacy of design. At least at the major intersections (4 or 5 in the Eastern Mass. area), clover leaf interchanges should be replaced with egress and entry ramps so that traffic merges into travel beyond other merging. Yes, million in cost. But think of the jobs created.

And . . . . put in the context of the original purpose of the interstate highway system -- national defense -- wouldn't such upgrade of such a strategic threat as gridlock traffic (ohmy god, what if there were terrorists coming during rush hour?!?!!) . . wouldn't it be an aspect of military funding??

Summer heat beats down upon the vast areas of black roofs and black pavements. Black is very heat-absorbent. Sometimes the heat is such that the tar or roofing compound softens, even bubbles.

But then it cools down.

What a waste!!!

Could there not be a grid of pipes atop the roofs, even fitted into slots cut in the parking lots? Within the pipes would be a heat absorbing fluid that would convey the heat deep underground into chambers containing huge vats.

Stored heat!!! For later use when pumped into circulation for buildings close enough. Kind of the opposite of the old-days of cooling when ice would be cut from ponds and stored in extremely insulated buildings where it would stay frozen until the next winter. In the interim, it would be cut for various cooling purposes.

Back then, foot-thick walls filled with sawdust were at least one of the insulating "technologies". With our modern materials we should be able to create a "collaborating alternative" of actual ice for cooling along with compressor-created chillers and refrigeration.

So, too, with heating from what the sun had heated but we'd stored away. Another resource of waste heat is significantly in some nuclear waste. This is contained (supposedly) in absolute safety from any radiation leakage. The temperature of the containers is almost dangerously high, and will remain so for extended periods of months, at least.

Rather than bury this "heat-resource" out in the middle of nowhere abandoned salt mines, shouldn't it be shipped to facilities where it could be used as heating?

So these might have to be very secure, monitored, even shielded buildings.

So think of the jobs created building them. Hooking up circulating jacket piping around the hot containers, connecting same to heat-distribution systems analogous (and in collaboration with) the steam-from-generator-plants that now heats at least parts of most major cities.

Re-usables and re-fillables.

Think the packaging. Think especially the plastic bottling.

Think, that even if recycled, the manufacturing energies and resources thereof are wasted when the object of such short "life" becomes something that has to be destructed to a certain state, then re-manufactured using, hopefully most of the remains of its previous incarnation (or in-carton-ation).

The carton could become analogous to the "pallet" upon which freight is transported. More and more pallets are specifically owned by pallet companies to whom they're returned after use. They're then re-leased (or whatever the arrangement) to the shipping outfits.

The same could be done to some extent with boxes. Cardboard might be replaced by some kind of plastic, strictly rectilinear shapes made slightly variant so the empty boxes could be nested for return to distribution centers from which they'd go out to subsequent shippers.

Massive amounts of essentially new (used just once) cardboard become recycled "waste", by the shipping container-full sent all the way across the seas for remanufacture in Asia. What a waste of the material and of the fuels to transport it globally.

Containers such as jugs should be refilled. The housewife goes to the store with her quart (or larger) container, deposits into the dispensing machine, and gets the milk, soda, whatever.

Simply, collectively (and that's the appropriate term), if not refilled by the consumer, containers of all kinds should be . . . collected for re-distribution to be filled by the producer. Especially wasteful in my estimation are motor oil jugs, heavy plastic, actually "new", that get not only thrown away but destroyed in the incinerator or buried in the landfill.

A combined container (boxes, bottles, jugs, and more) collection and re-distribution center would surely create a lot of jobs for the "low-end" wage-earner demographic. Considering that without such employment that group might have no alternative opportunity but to "collect", wouldn't it be better, even more economic, for the government to not only venture-capitalize, but, if necessary, ongoing subsidize this type of employment! Earning money! Preserving resources!

Those little tiny plastic water bottles . . . a couple sips of the Poland or Disani or whatever and they're empty and get tossed into the rubbish barrel (and end up in the landfill, but also, "decomposed to granular molecular components" in the terrestrial and especially marine environment . . . . .

Bad enough that in over half the world the population (mostly the women) have to walk long distances to obtain even impure if not dangerous water -- and in the "advanced" world we transport " designer-doses of H_2O interstate and even trans-oceanic. And here and in other "advanced" nations, the local water supplies are not only pure, but monitored, and fluoridated to prevent tooth decay.

But we internationally ship water, sip the water from the little plastic demitasses which we then toss in the rubbish barrel.

The town of Concord Mass (famous for the "shot heard 'round the world and notable for its elite and affluent populous) recently managed to pass an ordnance prohibiting the sale of bottled water in those little containers. I'm sure their perspicacity pervaded into other aspects of the water-waste such as I've mentioned above. But they could do something about this blatant waste of the container, at least. The precious free-market of plunder (resources for such transport) for profit (bottled water is expensive) itself was beyond even Concord's campaign to curtail.

But they got that ban on the bitty-bottles by. Resulting in snickers and scoffs and even scatologicals from the right-wingers. Not just in the local paper, Concord's conservation ethic was subject to ridicule in national media.

The Concordians, I'm sure, took all this as an inverse adulation in that the deprecations of their accomplishment derived from the demonstrably dolt demographic . . . quite the obverse of Democratic . . . .
.

At any rate, hardly a pittance of plastic saved, but every little bit of conservation helps. And they made a significant point to be pondered for those who are able. Ponder is somewhat an exponential neural connectivity ability beyond prattle.

And I pictured. . . . . .

Picture it with me . . . . .

"Welcome to Concord."

"I thank you. You've a fine town here, and famous."

"We do have a heritage, and still the bridge."

"Ah yes. The birth of our nation, one of the pangs here."

"Well put, Mr. Fran. . . "

"Ben. No need for such formality."

"Alright, Ben. Before I continue showing you around, perhaps you're thirsty."

"I could use a bit of quench."

"Right in here. This is our general store."

"The water dispenser?"

"Oh no, Ben. We got rid of such obsolescence long ago. We have individual portion containers. Here."

"So small, but the water looks quiet clear. Hmmm. . . the glass feels pliable, soft."

"It's 'plastic', Ben."

"Amazing. Yes, this water is good. But so little in the container."

"Here, have another."

"Thanks. That'll suffice, I think. Now where do I place these containers for further use?"

"Over there in that barrel."

"It's almost full with these containers already. When does someone come to refill them?"

"Oh, that refilling stopped long ago. We just throw these things away."

"Throw them away? There's nothing wrong with them!! Look, I even put the caps back on mine -- others have too -- why would anyone not preserve something . . . ."

"Not worth it. Too much trouble. We just dump them."

"That seems terrible. Ungodly. UnAmerican."

"But to make them is so cheap."

"What's cheap?"

"Oh, they're only worth about a penny.

And Ben Franklin realized the free-market driven economics of modernicity and proclaimed . . .

"A penny saved? That's all? Hell, **WASTE 'EM !!"**

The Fallacy of Free-Market Individualism

"Should" or "ought to" don't function here.

Yes, taking on a debt, be it a mortgage or otherwise, one *should* accurately calculate what he can afford to pay. The party *ought* to be responsible enough to not overextend herself. If a couple, they ought to, they should, be in charge of the private enterprise of their private "business" -- their income-to-expense balance even in projections of variables and viscissitudes.

Free-Market Individualism's standpoint would be that the actual locus of culpability for any economic crisis is . . . the people. their failure of "should-ing" and "ought to-ing".

These, the people of the general populace, I'll term "the former".

"The people" of the highest echelons of finance (institutions, raters thereof, regulators of both and beyond) . . . . these people "should" have and "ought to" have been not only responsible . . . . but given the mathematical formulas and hierarchy ("quants" etc.), synergized (or **sin**-ergized) by computerized computations -- these "people" were educated experts.

These, the people of the economics echelon, I'll term "the latter".

"The former" were computing their transactions not from some bygone era's simplistic notion of "common sense". For even back pre-credit days, "common sense" as the thought-function-default of the common-person would most likely be revealed as either an oxymoron . . . . or a *de-facto* status of not having leeway to exercise their common senselessness (such as a debt-based consumption of products and services has revealed -- which didn't exist back then in pre-credit days).

"The latter were, though, computing their transactions within an opening-ended paradigm. They were *creating* the economic system inclusive of consumer credit-debt as "inverse-collateral". Credit card thru swipe and the goods go with the purchaser. Implicit, and insidiously here, an economic system was established wherein the economic activities of "the former" were replaced by "the latter": buying by owing to . . . thus not only "inverse-collateral" involved, but a continuity-cost. Purchases far beyond cash-for (at any point of the half-century) were taken home with but the swipe of the card. "The latter", using as their equivalent of consensus-sense what their ascended positions and algorithms and projections otherwise provided them truly superseded "the former". Even to the extent that in many cases you can't use cash. Have to charge it on card.

"The latter", the people of economics controlled "The former", the plain people.

"The former", facing such a revolution of system, and revel-ation in immediate gratification (pay for it little-by-little later, they hoped . . . .), naturally availed themselves of fulfillments and even indulgence. That's human nature. Which, itself, supersedes that mythic mentality -- common sense. For neo-common sense was overwhelmingly, constantly, brainwashingly pummeling the people to perform what the pinnacles of prominence (the GDP Cartel) were promulgating. Common sense now was to take advantage of what the experts advise and provide.

"The latter" (experts) through their dimension of a mythic "common sense in securitizations" (and debt-swaps and derivatives and all) had established what seemed to be a roaring economy. People were financially enabled, thus spending/buying, thus manufacture and travel and other life-amenities were making money, making jobs available. That debt was collateral for such significant levels of economic activity was a synergy!! Interest!!! On time-span payments. And, worst come to worst (for the debtor), maybe best come to best for the return to the lender. Maxed-up level of interest rate ever onward until either final payout/seizure . . . . or default (in which case the write-off to the lender represented a sort of inverse inverse-collateral. The unpaid debt addend became a subtractant from balance sheet and probably a tax advantage. And when "the latter" came to the point of not even holding the debt instruments???? Here was the elixir! The philosopher's stone. Bundle debt and sell it!!!! Sell segments of it, selected and spliced according to some kind of bond or share or buyer thereof. And just in case, take out insurance so that actual loss would be hedged and might (given the slight-probability-of-cataclysm vs. low premium costs) even yield profit! From loss!!

"The latter" (big business and banks and such) created such a hybrid of high finance and high jinx, based on hierarchies: experts, extrapolations of data, algorithms, cyber-computing/conflating/interfacing data for buy-sell instantaneity -- the *profit* production an addend to the "*income*" pool from people-transactions' payments.

"The former" (the populace) . . . anyone would expect their level of calculating abilities (yes, double entendre), let alone math to deal with their end of this brave new world? Hardly. The experts couldn't even grasp it all.

Especially regarding mortgages.

I've read quite a number of times in the last month or so -- that the complexity of mortgage math was even beyond those in the business. No longer did a bank loan money, buyer owe to bank, and a 30-year constancy created carry on. Just from consideration of mortgage multiplicity (variable rates, negative inceptions, pre-pay terms, etc. etc.) it was no longer a bank's having a simple ledger on its mortgagee. When the banks came to sell up/down the line, their "common sense" of what "should" and "ought to" be their criteria for a borrower's eligibility . . . . became somewhat, so soon, a non-issue. As for the big-bank institutions that up-sucked the illusory fertilization of these little squiggles of valuation, so complex had globalization become, that only few even of those up in the Elysian Fields of finance saw that the impressive swell of portfolios was . . . .an overheated Ponzi-pregnancy of the whole economic system. Not a breeding bonanaza.

And of the few who sensed . . . . it was mostly their intuition as evidentiary element. Not even they had ACTUAL PROOF (documentation). . . . . even of Madoff.

For what can be derived from derivatives but a squaring of the eventual approach to zero?? . . . . one . . . *singularity* sensation . . . . . .da-data-data. . da. . . daaa . . .

So, simply, the highest levels of expertise didn't do their "should " or "ought to". So why assume the rank and file of risk and finance would have the means to measure all the ramifications and rampantifications of the economy? Of course they couldn't.

But more to a point, if not the point. They didn't. Neither "The former" nor "The latter" acted wisely. In part, this was because "wisdom" is an "Heisenbergian construct". There's the ongoing *"uncertainty"* of whether one point's wisdom will be such at another point of economo-socio-space/time. Also, one's wisdom is so often not another's even unto the differential perspective seeming "idiocy".

And here we get back again to a term I used right at the beginning of this diatribe. "Free-market individualism".

Whether of "The former" or "The latter", an absolutely free market process may become a paradigm of pure possessiveness (MY WAY OR NO WAY). For one's free marketeering maneuvers and even malfeasances represent to him his dog-eat-dog Darwinian superiority if not supremacy. An absolutely free market is not absolutely free for its mass of members. At least it becomes not (and started out as not -- from Genghis *et al* all through Feudalism and former Baronial times even in the U. S.). Established systems from conquering hordes to cornered markets enslave, enserf, or ensnare, not free the general populace.

And, further, that which is (has become) a controlling Carnegie, cartel, corporation, or other private-enterprise "entity" is actually the **governing** system of its concern (mining, manufacture, railroads, even derivatives) and far beyond (raw resources through processing vs. competition plus profit).

Thus the private enterprise is the government if we remove government itself!!!!

Removing government itself takes from the market and social and economic and ecologic equation of action and interaction almost everything other than the closed-circuit quest of the private enterprise -- bottom-line. Well, top line, too, has become pretty much a priority: how many millions the CEO gets or walks away with even when dismissed.

People comprise the actual government.

People is the "management" (and above) of private enterprise.

People of government represent an input ratio (or dimension) deriving from diverse levels, interests, demographics, etc. . . . as well as those who act as liaisons for the interests, principals, principles (and lack thereof) of the private sector.

People of private sector (primarily "corporate") governance are hugely less diverse in their concerns, which are overwhelmingly to make profits, to profit from the making in their own upper-level incomes and options.

People of government, though including a spectrum from diverse demographics and economics, aren't representative of any rabble or eco-nut or socialism-seeking subversion of free enterprise/Capitalism. A significant number of those in Congress have been and are quite wealthy: and for many years now, what with oversight and controls, they didn't get rich from "brown-bagging", from K-Street-direct-deposits, and certainly not from their salaries. Most of those who are rich came from riches. Others (Clinton, an admirable example of achievement on merit or at least intelligence/charisma/etc -- forget personal ethics, of course) . . .others made government their private enterprise thru perseverance and prominence (but that required the backing and fund-fronting of others).

From the Founding Fathers through the Roosevelts and Kennedys and Bushes and maybe inclusive of Mitt, the very leaders of the country have significantly been backed by "dynasty". Presidents, especially of late, have run on the financing of major private enterprises and people (greater than grass-roots pittances). From Soros to Adelson, the mega-contributions. From Exxon, HP, Tyson, Cargill, Caterpillar, ... the major private industry input . . . . thus investment in . . . . thus obligation *by* government's people to promote the purposes of those who provided the "venture capital" of these upstarts' political startups and ongoing political careers!

But at least the people of the government include many who take into even priority account the value that environment, education, medicine, foods, sanitation, and such represent as the whole population's survival; but actual national detriment though if allowed to deteriorate or diminish.

The people of private industries have traditionally not shared such survey, nor much given a shit how much shit their processes have produced, piled, percolated, or even poisoned!!

The diverse-dimension of government's personnel protects people per se. Thus there have been rules established for workplace safety, wage levels, benefits, etc. To recognize that "labor" is actually the "capital of Capitalism" (without it who would make or do what makes the money secondarily? . . . But job security added to things enumerated just above) just doesn't appear clearly in the *fundamentalist* perspective of free-market milieu.

From Forbes, August 20, 2012. Excerpts: (here, a case of *extremist* . . .)

> *"Americanism means individualism, but 'Hire American' is collectivist, urging businesses to pay more just to patronize 'our guys'. This is not rational patriotism, it is not Americanism, it is primitive tribalism.*
>
> *Purchasing labor services abroad, if it saves money, is beneficial to every-one, including American workers. Outsourcing does not destroy American jobs, it simply changes the kind of work Americans specialize in. If fewer Americans need to work in manufacturing, then more Americans will be*

hired in nonmanufacturing jobs. That's The Law of Comparative Advantage,
covered in any decent economics text . . . . ."
" . . .A Congressional Medal of Honor should go to the CEO who cuts
his costs the most, whether he does it by outsourcing or any other means."
"Outsourcing Is The U.S. At Its Best"
Harry Binswanger - Capital Flows

Maybe, were there other jobs . . . . but unless the unemployment level since the start of the "Great Recession" of late is a lie, . . . there aren't!! Here.

And even there? The offshores to which almost our whole national heavy industry and manufacturing sailed during the last decades? Unless there's an economic "surge" so that spending can resume here (spending = buying), will there be a decrease in the selling there and thus of the need to manufacture over there?? And if there is an economic "surge" here, will it be Trojan horse precursor for emergent insurgent inflation? Or/also just another bubble of irrational exuberance . . . to burst/bust?? Here and there and everywhere global?

Free market individualism by "The former" or "The latter" needs an operant level, leeway, yes, but with controls. By others than the "marketeers" themselves.

For despite what "should" be or "ought to" be, obviously things didn't work out that way and wouldn't again if unfettered free-for-all market manias ensue again.

Private party "free market individualism" is but naiveté significantly due to the complexity of our economy and its divisions, devices, divisiveness, deviances, diversions, derivatives. It was (at least) not ignorance or irresponsibility alone to account for some-one's taking out a high-point or variable-jump mortgage when the ongoing-seemingly-to infinity of real estate values meant that by getting into the property at point A, it could be re-financed at point B and yield cash appreciation for whatever . . . . or just flipped.

Free market individualism, operated from its position of "wisdom" (taking advantage of opportunity's "operant-spectrum", by which I mean a projected period of time in which further moves would prove profitable to the individual) . . . . free market individualism took out the usurious rate "sub-prime" loans, primarily for rewrites!!! Not initial property purchases. Not alone from the mortgage/loan company's spiel was there influence. There was the evident. Bi-part. Who cares if you're paying extra 6% when your property's going to soar up 18%, given the proof of trend. And what the actual investors were doing.

On the one hand, many were pulling out equity, even debt-equity, to play the housing market. On the other hand, some who re-mortgaged were doing so to initially lower payments and thus hang onto their troubled property at least until things would improve for them. And on a third hand, a whole retired demographic was picking up and moving to better climes such as Florida's and assuming that even if their health shit hit the fan, at least they'd always be able to sell their homesite for at least what they'd paid.

From my reading, semi-extensive, it seems that mortgages given at the behest of Fannie or Freddie and creating "nightmares on Elm -- and every other -- St.) in order to give destitute minorities their own piece of earth (not quite "Jeffersonian" pie)* . . .seems that wasn't the case.
*as in "The Jeffersons"

Countrywide and others semi-autonomous from Fed Reg, often in collusion with StateReg because of bank pressures, their vast volume of subprime, and actually "toxic" mortgages were the re-mortgaging for and of a diverse demographic. Think how many McMansion-scale defaults, such as in Vegas, or Condos in Miami!! Gated communities with squatters now infiltrating and now peeing in the algae-clogged swimming pools. Not to many American-dream aspirant *indigents* were those loans rigged/written!! The housing collapse (which took along with it much else) didn't result from do-gooder "a home and an acre" (in "Reconstruction the promise was a mule and an acre . .) out-pouring of socialistic idealism or blatant voter-baiting. It was economy's systemic failure.

Had the plain people of free market individualism projected all the possibilities, probabilities, paranoid protectionism of their selves would have usurped the rather incredible economic growth from post WWII up until just those few years ago. There would have been a "preemptive recession", so to speak.

At least to me, from my perspective, "should" and "ought to" have included such dire possibilities as losing a job, house value decrease, and other incentives for me to invest in playing it safe by not playing at all!! My economic advisors consider my stance with almost bemused annoyance. Were I not so "conservative", they'd make a lot more off me. And I might make a lot more off me. But I don't take chances of losing a whole lot (even if not all) to possibly make even quite a bit more (than I actually did: Enron, Lucent, etc.)

But heaven forbid the rest of the people were all as careful and frugal as I.

But, heaven help us, for it was the aspiration to affluence and the acting thereon that:

    Brought about the great growth of the economy of the last decades
        even inclusive of the off shoring labor and attrition-to-big-box
        of *really* private prior enterprises so much
    Brought the whole astoundingly complex complex down, analogous to how
        an "immune complex" can devastate an organism. An "immune complex"
        forms by the integral binding of an antibody to an antigen, and when deposited
        in an organ results in disease (such as lupus, erythematosis, rheumatoid
        arthritis, scleroderma, and others).
            Do we all see how "bundling" into derivatives resembles the just-above?
            In investment organs of the economic "body"???
                Frankenstein monsters, monetary . . .?
Ultimate expertise failed to foresee, forestall.

Greenspan himself advocated letting market forces do the corrective determinations.

The hierarchy of institutions were divided between absolute scoundrels of originators, and the bastions of international banking who bought the bundles, having bought into the extrapolations and projections of their high-level experts, algorithms, transaction-instantaneity (to "correct" for "blips") . . . . and AIG on call if fail else all.

****

Another, almost obverse, perspective of "free market individualism".

Regarding "The former." (the populace).

The people, the overall distribution and demographic of the supposed 90% hold the assumed 2% wealth of the nation (somewhere around there, considering that, like one point something percent of the population is held to control some 90 plus % of the wealth.)Yes, include in the 90% "people" those who get welfare, food stamps, WIC, and other perhaps more entitled entitlements (such as for legitimate disabilities and for unemployment, etc.)

Whatever "The former" (the general population) brings in . . . goes right back out. To the mortgage or landlord, to the grocer or pharmacy, the car payment or rapid transit, the cable and phone bills, to booze stores, to clothing and furnishing and even frivolity now and then here and there (amusement park or something) . . . . everything that they derive "from the system" (be it from wages or "dole") goes right back in.

EVERYTHING. Who, on the population-breadth level, has anything leftover?

So even the "entitlements", after an in-one-hand-and-out-the-other of the recipient, ultimately/rapidly revert into the economy. And into the tax base into which those pay --those to whom the recipient has paid for whatever substance or service.

Recirculation. Pour-up even from trickle-down?

Free market individualism of "The former" (the population) does not amass wealth, thus extract it from the economy. (Only at an economic level of homeowner is there a form of wealth-accretion. This is equity, which is not amassing or extracting from the economy. Obviously it's just a "deferred payment paradigm". And, less so obvious, property appreciation is not an economic substantive until acted upon, "cashed-in" etc. As we've seen, even almost exponential appreciation is but a construct!! A conspiracy?)

To look at economy as a system of circulation, its procedures and processes can be recognized as scientific, technological. If a vast vessel (population group) obtaining disbursement from the economy . . . . returns it all back into the economy via cost of living etc. . . . . . what's happening to the "reservoir" being emptied?

To look and see that this vast sub-system just recirculates what flows into it, one should be led to look elsewhere for what's become the demonstrable dessication.

Free market individualism of "The latter" (the economics echelon) is a fair focus for finding out where the fault may lie. It seems not so much a leak is the problem. No, it's more like 1) an evaporation

The recent "debt-standard" (securitized whatevers) was a collateral basis for purchasing, accreting, incurring. From the credit card to the home equity loan to the tranch-tailored derivatives, to the influence-inflated credit raters' ratings . . . . . the overheat of exuberance (actually, mania) created "steam-liquidity". And it evaporated!

But it also significantly 2) involves a "big-suck scenario".

In the "distribution of wealth" in this country (hell, in the world, actually), it's obvious that the major "entitlement" is taken out of the overall economy to provide for multi-million dollar incomes for that elite few. Only a portion of that goes back into . . the economy . . . for a substantial amount is retained up in the high-end, highly restricted "eddy" of elitist economic circulation.

Any argument that "they" have "earned" their "free market individualism" demands for limitless riches poses disproportion as deserved dispensation. The Darwinian (actually somewhat an inapt term) success of someone should not equate with a supremacy that extracts excess even just within the closed-context of the guy himself. Someone who can earn $5 million a year just might be able to find enjoyment by getting by on keeping just $2 million after paying into some context of value and responsibility and "should" and "ought" rather than almost autistic self-centricity!!

When what we've assumed as America's success as a nation, society, people, is being closed (parks, police and fire stations, highway rest areas) -- terminated (school athletic and arts programs, elder care transportation and facilities) -- laid off (public works employees including teachers, varied private enterprise personnel in down-sizings) -- and more . . . .)

What's happened to what was providing for these aspects of our American values, ethics, our American. . .way . . of. . . life . . .?

The majority of immigrants have come, legally or illegally, into this country to work. And the majority do. The "Hispanic" varietal-influx? Check out hotels and freight docks and anything else blue collar . . and more and more are upward mobile with training and education. Within a couple generations from now the Hispanic should be no more looked on as some alien (or sedition) element than came to be the Italians and Irish (who were horrendously even hated back in the late 1800s and into early 1900s).

Not the "lower classes". Not the broad population demographic. Not the immigrants. to blame. Until eight or nine years ago there was no "problem unemployment" level. Not the other minorities. It's only the minor minority of any of these who really suck off the system, sequentially sometimes, generation after generation. Once considered human "constitutional" defects (or "bad blood") by the Eugenics Movement -- this demographic fraction is the result of what I call "Transgenetic inheritance of their environment", now actually a scientific area termed "epigenetics". Again, though, even the free-loaders unload whatever dole they get right back up into the totalic economic flow.

Yes, some "should". Some "ought to".

Especially "The latter" atop the ladder. Ought to be responsible to more.

Yes, so many are. And were it not for those at the top (who don't shut-off their concept of "success" at a "glass bottom" below which they'd not deign to disperse their largesse) . . . were it not for many of the @379 billionaires in this country (recent Forbes -- and god knows how many probably thousands of millionaires) . . . there wouldn't be culture, charity, hospital wings, art stipends, the opera, much of PBS funding (although the majority thereof now seems to require that the "P" stand for "Private", especially "P" as in Prominent corporations paying the way).

And any idea of actual <u>wealth</u> distribution would be even more suicidal than the recent attempts at amassing "wealth through transmutations". The reservoirs, cisterns, tanks, and even varied vessels of "capital" are indispensable for the hydraulic system of our economy to function fully. And dividing up the wealth totally would provide everyone with hardly a good day's pay . . . . and just be an interim within the process that would result in, again, wealth <u>dys</u>tribution. And the means for that end are absolute requisites for our system (Capitalism) and for those most successful (Capitalists).

But the cyclic *cumulative* end-result, as at present, results in hardships for so many, yet excessive affluence for so few,

The profits of American corporations, as at present, result in losses of jobs which would pay the willing. And even into which some of the lesser willing would be mandated to work to earn their keep. But offshore labor is just soooo cheaper . . . thus our bottom line so higher and managers' millions so morer.

And "free market individualism" is, after all, the infrastructure of the free market economy. The person is the individual. His performance his primacy, his prestige, his portfolio, and even port for his yacht.

But what about his country? His countrymen?

In both "The former" (us-es) but especially "The latter" (the thems) shouldn't there be a priority beyond personal? Beyond primacy?

Should there not, too, be "**free market identificationalism**" -- that one identifies with others? Empathy. Caring. Sharing. Making sure the system works for all?

For what are the alternatives?

Drastically cut social security? With an imminent immensifying old age population?

Go back to pre-Obama and let millions have no health insurance?

Cut off welfare programs and let them beg in the streets or starve
Let there be homeless, who cares from the co-ops and Conn.claves?
(There have been alternatives…seen most often in French history . . . and Russian . . .)

Should". "Ought to".
Almost beside the points above.
The point to those points will be what will result if our lack of caring is the stimulus for what effect it will be the cause!!!
It's a matter of, yes, cause and effect. Not right or wrong. Not should or ought.
And those crowds who could become the madding, the maddened, must, themselves, be recognized as a potential portrayal of <u>their</u> perspective of . . . . thus their valid enactment of their free market individualism . . . .

AND FINALLY A FEW PAGES OF MISCELLANY

Regarding the Middle East's oil.

Part of the "foreign oil" America uses comes from OPEC.
OPEC nations are Islamic, thus consider Christianity a blasphemy,
     denounce democracy as a heresy.
Blasphemy and heresy are Satanic and the destruction of their
     adherents will be rewarded. Such is the view of many
     Islamic fundamentalists, even the quest of extremists.
     And for oil we pay money to them???

Almost all of the revenue of the OPEC countries comes from oil
The drilling/extraction of that oil, as well as significant (if not pre-
     ponderant) revenue derives from Western (esp. American)
     petrochemical companies and Western nation consumption
     of refined petro-products.
The distribution of OPEC wealth provides extreme, ostentatious
     wealth for the elite, while leaving the vast majority of the
     population rather, if not actually, impoverished, suppressed,
     unemployed, and worse.
          Thus the Mideast kingdoms and their myriad privileges and
          princes depend upon a Western presence, not only petro-
          financially, but "existentially". The West is both potential
          protector from popular uprising and provision of funds for
          protracted, projected dynastic enrichment.

What "trickle-down" economic enhancement provides
for the populace derives from Western capital infusion for
oil extraction.

Payments to OPEC are a *quid pro quo* for that aspect of popular suppres-
sion (by royalty) which protects Western petrochemical facilities and
equipment, as well as product. Termination of Western capital into

OPEC would end our collusion with their ruling echelon, further
impoverish their people (think Iraqi sanctions), and result in revved
rage readings (religious and otherwise).
Cessation of Western payments for, and usage of, OPEC oil would result
in replacing the prevalent infusion from, influence by, and power
(geo-political and potential military) of other countries such as
Russia, China . . . even India.

Therefore, to resolve any dilemma regarding OPEC oil . . . .

We should: 1)
Stop trading with bastards that don't like us and our religion
and show them how much they need us and are helpless
(or hopeless) without us. (What else would Jesus do??)
Use up all our reserves first, for we alone will set the price so
much cheaper and thus enable such increased usage
for such factorial short-term profits.
Thus postpone eventual need to resume OPEC derivation/
extraction which Russia and China and even India will
have exploited fully . . . . but of course will share so
cooperatively with us . . . .with U. S.
We should: 2)
Do none of the above.

We should continue the present paradigm of oil production, propping-up and proxy-postulate positioning of emirates (etc.), populace/extremist controls, etc. as we have been for years.

For in the Middle East, our presence and even our payments represent an investment in a global-domain socio-politi-economic conflation of control, thus their, and our, national security.

The petro-resources derived are actually but the "interest" we derive from that kind of globalized-investment portfolio.

We might "profit" more . . . . . but at what cost?

Regarding your oil

Points to ponder.

My term "oil" here is a generic which includes not only petroleum, but gas, and includes, the various "geologic containments" (shale, etc.)

You buy and sell oil from a global market combining specific resources of Canada, Norway, Venezuela, Africa, OPEC, U. S. (already), and more.

From the oil you buy, you sell branded petroleum products and are making "windfall profits".

You have oil under **your** land -- which you also farm.

You already drill, pump, and significantly profit from your "domestic" reserves.

Your agricultural activities and survival otherwise depend upon the purity, even potability, of the water under your land.

Obviously, you're aware that drilling, fracking, etc. entail risk of
     Leaks or other contamination of the land and underlying aquifer/wells.
You have only so much oil under your land. One projection is 100 years'
     reserve. That would take care of two generations' of your lineage.

     You should: 1)

          Drill and pump as much of your own oil as fast as
             you can so that it can be sold cheaper and
             thus consumed faster especially as gasoline in
             automobiles.

          Sell this "domestic" reserve into the International
             petro-pool, thus lowering market prices so
             that the burgeoning consumer masses of
             China and India (and soon, elsewhere) can
             use more and more and more of everyone's
             oil reserves

     You should: 2)

          I think, obviously, do none of the above. Bad enough with mere
products, but to advocate increasing production for the sake of stimulating more consumption . . of any
natural resource . . . is akin to anarchy!! As for lower price as proportionate to pumping volume or
specific source . . . . . . hah.

Alternativation . . .

First, summary of last: "Your own oil" – one of last week's emails.
Instead of oil, think of the commodity as food. You only have so much.
You depend on your supply for your survival, and for monetary profit.
Would you lower the price in order to sell a lot more in a hurry and thus,
    the sooner, use up the limited supply you have?
Given alternative "routes", would you insist upon running a pipeline
    across your food-source, knowing the chance of leakage? Remember,
    "footprints" such as the little Valdez in the great big ocean and the

Tiny-er BP drilling rig in the Carribean . . . . footprings "BLEED" . . . .
   (Under the contested pipeline route is a major aquifer)
The "conservatives' " compulsion to drill, drill, drill is but one of the many
   areas of advocating exploitation of the irreplaceable, for the sake of
   mere monetary (and momentary) gain

And now, to the first of this weekend's . . . .
   Concerning Alternative Energy   (by AHSchneider)

There are several fuels/systems being researched/developed
         Solar, wind, wave, plant-based, algae-based, hydrogen cell
            and even others I'd term "esoterics"
No one of these will likely ever provide for even **all** the *stationary* electrical
         needs of developed countries, let alone providing charge for mobile
         electrical demands (cars, trucks).
Even the combination of all these may not suffice for heavy industrial
         demands (such as smelting, electroplating, production welding,
         and large electric motor-powered manufacturing or mining
         processes.

At present, solar and wind seem to be viable systems for limited power
         generation – but the costs associated are greater than for petro-
         or gas-fueled generating facilities.
There is no *certainty* that wave, algae, even fuel cell energy derivation
         will become market-feasible.
There may always be "conventional grid" electrical requirements for the
         population, not just for its industry and production demands. So
         there may be an open-ended time frame in which petroleum or
         gas resources are of ultimate and absolute necessity.

Given that "foreign oil" is part of what the U.S. uses may be part of why the
         price is high.
Paying OPEC countries for oil is like indulging the (Islamic) enemy.

Not exploiting all our domestic reserves in order to provide our people
        with cheap automotive fuel so they can use more by traveling
        more . . . is unpatriotic, anti-capitalistic.

We should: 1)
    Mourn that Newt Gingrich didn't get his chance to lower the price of
gasoline to $2.50-something a gallon so everyone could splurge on con-
sumption, within a couple generations use ours up all of ours.
    Shut off OPEC oil. That way we'll be so much safer when the rulers
no longer have our petro-wealth and our "proxy-protection" . . . and the
populace, thus reduced to actual starvation, would have even more rabid
reasons to attack us
    Make sure whoever we elect will disregard all the treasonous "market-
globalism" and also the nonsense about our domestic environment and drill
and frack all the oil and gas wherever it is and whatever the result because
it'll boost consumption thus lower price (supply-demand ratio). And
put people to work. A few. For little while.
    Make sure that even sequential venture capital funding is allocated to
start-ups of shoe-sales, coffee-shops, hamburger chains, boutique wine-
sample websites, and such. Profit-taking from share-value increments
of such "second-wave dot.coms" make any matter of eventual cash-flow
rather secondary in the paradigm of investment-to-return priority for the
in-group who know when to bail out.
    Don't back "boondoggles" like Solectra or Evergreen Solar, with
combined VC, or (heaven forbid) any government subsidy to keep the
industries and jobs in this country through the development period
until they'd achieve self-sustaining financial state. And such potential
strategic survival industries (as opposed to subs and sips, etc.) present

the possibility of becoming major employers.

As for biofuels etc., conservatives view such innovations as imaginations'   delusions.

As stated in Forbes Mag.. . . "we live in a world or oil . . . ."
.........projections are
for 100 years' domestic reserves (U.S.) – and
as said above, that's only 2 generations.
Then what?

But (concluding 1),

We should use all of ours. Drill, buy, and burn American!!!
When our supply has been depleted we don't have to worry about from whom will come our energy resources. We'll be dead then. Screw the future. Even our great-grand children. After all, what did any of them ever do for us???

But seriously
Or we should: 2)

Realize that some alternatives may not ever be viable.

That even all alternatives may not provide all needs

That we may always need to draw from whatever
petroleum/gas sources are available.

Realize that we have resource-reserves, and proven means to
drill, frack, and otherwise extract – and to process
into fuels and other petro-chemical products

Realize that we should by all means preserve our safety:

By preserving **our own** resources for the future. For now,
we should continue drawing from the multi-nation
petro-pool..

By maintaining a politico-economic/détente reciprocity with
OPEC, and even Mr. Chavez.

By actually providing for the survival, if not also the semi-Westernization, of OPEC-country populace through our petro-presence of (personnel other than Arab, and the concomitant subtle "insurgence" of Western culture). . . . as well as the $$$s.

Conclusion: don't blow through your own by making it cheap and then you got no choice, let alone control, over the other guys' resources!!!!!!

.

10/19/12

regarding an article from
PROVIDENTIAL
PERSPECTIVE
vol. 26, No. 2, September, 2012   The Teaching Journal of
The Providence Foundation

Obama, Romney, Other: Who Should Christians
Vote for in the 2012 Election?
Including Biblical Qualifications
for Civil Leaders

by Stephen McDowell

Copy of article at end of . . . . .
Herewith, **my** comments.

"Our Founders put us on a Biblical path that enabled us to become the most free, just, prosperous, charitable, and virtuous nation the world has ever seen."
What?? Perhaps Mr. McDowell should read more than his Bible whilst listening to AM radio.

Consider how charitable the original distribution of land between those first here: the English, the French, the Spanish. *"Yea, verily as Jesus would have us, let us divide the 'loaf of land' amongst ourselves so that all can be fed with property."*

Consider how justly, how "Jesusly", were treated those to whom this continent had been heritage and home. *"And I say unto thee, any amongst ye who are not of the skin color of ye, ye may send forth from thy midst into the winter of Deer Island even though they profess to have joined the faith of ye."* (Look how charitable and virtuous the "praying Indians" were treated). Most of those thus exiled to that Boston Harbor island starved or froze to death. The self-protection/self-survival concerns of the settlers (even professing-assimilated Indians a possible subversive, murderous threat) could have been dealt with less cruelly).

Our Founders' original intention was that the rights (including vote) were for those who were male, white, and owners of land. And our Founders so respected the Christian equality of mankind's rights to freedom and pursuit of happiness etc. under God . . . . unless they happened to be non-male/Protestant/"wealthy" . . . or, especially, owned by someone, including most of our Founders. The recent issue of *Smithsonian* contains an article concerning Jefferson and his slave-ownership (and "co-habitation-ship"). His "moral" reaction to "the peculiar institution" never prevented his owning, even allowing harsh discipline, of this "proto-capitalistic" labor force for his estate and enterprises. But from initial ethical reservations, he eventually realized that slaves, as the product produced by slaves . . provided more profit than his slave-labored agricultural or nail-making enterprises. And he proceeded Capitalistically on that premise.

And the while of these earlier decades, even as European countries quit the trade, America (North and South both) continued this so-profitable, hardly virtuous, commerce . . . . . Biblical?? well, maybe O.T., but surely not within the approbation of Jesus and the N. T.

Ongoing while the black skin population increased to pretty-much self-replication without further expense for importation . . . the red skin bunch were not really prospering under, at this point, subsequent leaders of this *"most free, just, . . .charitable, and virtuous nation"*. This continent was <u>populated</u> by "Indians" at the beginning of the 19th century. By the end, essentially a genocide had been committed (involving battle-related massacres, but also ethnic-cleansing forages rewarded by differential payments to the white "settlers" (or other) for male, female, or child scalp. (The attrition/wipeout was from some few millions of aboriginal peoples to a final @250,000, herded from their homeland to the "proto-concentration camps" called reservations.

How Nazi, not Christian!!!!

So Christian, so Jesus-like, the mid-and-onward into early 20th century welcome *(kind of "let the children of other nations come unto me")* welcome of the Irish, Italians, Southern European and Eastward Jews. So virtuous and charitable the conditions in New York City where burnings-alive, even breakings-on-wheel took place, where the filth piled save for what the roaming pigs ate, where people lived in tenements, the basements of which would be intermittently flooded by overflowing privies in the back yards -- yet a prominent Protestant church (I think Trinity) was one of the major property owners. And so obvious the God-blessed absence of any cursed socialistic-sin that would have taken from the ultra-rich (one of whom spent millions on his daughter's NY wedding), another whose daughter's betrothal to European nobility required a "dowry" of millions allocated to the refurbishment of Blenheim.

Gee, isn't there something in the Bible about a rich man not having much chance of getting into heaven?

Gee, can't you picture it? Jesus. Bread. The crowd beyond. And Jesus did break the bread and maybe one of the disciples said something socialistic like, *"I think some of these people are hungry"*. And Jesus broke the bread and rebuked Barack and saith unto him and the others, *"This is Capital expansion, profit. We can make a fortune on "food-stuff alchemy" that it seems I'm able to do. This'll work with fishes too!! We got the potential for a mass market here, guys. As for those people, why aren't they working rather than hanging around out here? We don't need no welfare state . . . ."*

Or picture the old lady with the coin and she's about to put it in . . .

"STOP!!!!!" That's your wealth. Which isn't really a significant wealth. But at least you have the potential to invest it to get some kind of dividend, some time hence with a dot.com a quick cash-out share appreciation (who cares if there's ever any actual cash flow??) Keep your wealth. God wants you to not distribute."

And having left historic New York . . .we come to more recent Washington . .

Ah, Ronald Reagan. The Man of God. Kind of a quasi-cousin to Jesus, the Son of God? Reagan *thought we were going "in the wrong direction and attempted to change course".*

To a considerable extent, Reaganomics may have represented the true first fruition of the credit-based bubble that finally burst so recently. Sure, things took off and boomed and people worked and earned and bought and bought more than they earned (on credit) so there could be even more manufacture and production than the actual, substantive basis of a market stability. Also, this was still the era of post-WWII development of devices and technologies. Also increase of population.

As for "trickle-down"? Seems somewhat a restriction of necessary monetary flow into the vast pool of . . . consumer-demographic!! Which means the vast population of lower income people who purchase things and services and stuff otherwise. The operant obverse of "trickle-down" is "held-up" economics, yes rewarding ambition and innovation and even exploitation and greed (which are absolutely necessary components of a successful socio-economic system . . . and I'll use the term "Darwinian" too. How obviously from history, absolute socialism, especially Communism, doesn't work. Aspiration and competition and reward are indispensable).

But when "trickle-down" allows multi-million dollar *incomes* to be so disproportionately retained (relative to the nothing that's left for the vast majority to be able to save, let alone horde) . . . . the while schools are without supplies, parks are untended, police and firemen laid off, libraries closed, millions without health care, sporadic areas of actual malnutrition . . . . . it's not only un-Christian!!! It sucks the sustenance out of the broad economic system (enterprises and jobs).

The vast wealth "held-up" primarily circulates only in the "high-end" high end. Biblical? Christian?

"Thou shalt beat thy plows into sword-shares". * No cuts of military budget.

Get rid of all the myriad "socialistic" programs that this country has established in order to provide for its *"people, the sheep of its pastures"*, so to speak. The list of Mitt's intended cuts and deletions represents a flaying of the flesh, a disembowelment of the organism, of what America has come to represent as a Christian concept nation. This "concept" obviously includes feeding the hungry, clothing the naked, healing the sick, "Samaritanish" stuff to help others. Educating the children. Providing for the security of the elderly. Etc. Etc. Etc. *Mitt's a Joel man (3/10 -- not an Isaiah (2:4) or Micah (4:3).

So, if anyone gets his subsidy or assistance reduced, he should compensate for the loss with dividend income or share-price increment cash-in. Buy military-industrial-complex stock!!!!

How crippling, FDR's polio. Worse, his "sincialistic" (sinful-socialistic) programs such as social security!! Wouldn't we be so much better off had Deuteronomy 1:13 been heeded *("Choose wise and discerning and experienced men")*, and as advocated, instead of SS, all had put all into Wall Street?

Notwithstanding the OT entitlement *"have dominion over"* and mandate *"go forth and subdue"*, it seems that Biblical, especially Christian Biblical requirement would be that man respect, preserve, maintain that which God has provided him. Such just might include the earth upon which he lives. Its resources as treasures, not quick-buck mass-market products for exploitation, excess utilization, and conversion to waste and pollution.

So virtuous our Founding Fathers and those who followed in their *footprints* upon the ethnic-cleansed, clear-cut, crop-depleted, super-fund-polluted, even riparian-combustive (several cases) desecration of what God hath created.

The "performance of recitation or ritual or such" or the "alarmism of approaching Armageddon" -- are these the criteria of being God-loving or God-fearing? Is the adherence to the specific schism's self-sanctity-assumption to be "of God" the requisite for really being "of God"? Thus, the Catholic is not Godly to the Protestant but the Methodist is not to the Baptist but the Lutheran is not to the Pentacostal but the other Evangelical is not Godly to the . . . . . and of course, the Jews are out of the God-loop entirely except where Israel represents a sort of "1st nation" logistical preemption over all others; also in their own self-to-God relationship-primacy.

Mitt will drill, baby, drill. On the land and on the sea.

Great idea. And God saith, *"suck all that oil out, and the coal, the Nat'l gas. Get it soon as you can because that'll make jobs for people because jobs pay wages and wages go into the free market system which is my other $pecial Creation from which profits derive and investor portfolios expand and many (though the few) get richer and richer".*

Great idea to use up our proven reserves (projected to last for the next 200 years!!! -- hardly more than 2 generations). These have proven means for extraction (drill, frack, etc.) and conversion into fuels. Perhaps these should remain as our reserves? And in the meantime we should, along with the other countries in the world, participate in using up each others'? And implement alternatives!!

Or should we introduce a Monroe Doctrine "circuit-breaker" system/syndrome on any and all internationalism, even though that's now a "set" of which *domesticism (American market/economy)* is a subset?

Great idea to vastly expand the availability of finite resources to lower the price so more people will use more so it will be used up in even less time. And meanwhile we'll stop buying from those other countries (such as actually minority supplier OPEC) and when our revenues for their oil no longer provide an income to their nations they'll love us the more, respecting our self-sufficiency?

Mitt's going to build that pipeline. Right over an aquifer. What the hell, what's to worry about water when it would cost more to re-route the oil (which I understand to be the main opposition -- the route of the pipe). But we need to get right on it. Not wait. For with some (is it) 23 million people out of work, between the oil rigs and the pipe line we'll get them all back on the job. . . . . . .??

Mitt. Multi-millionaire. Obviously thus in a position to network, combine, collaborate, joint-venture with others of that echelon.

Mitt. Market forces man. Get demon government out of things. Saint Private Sector solely and singly for salvation.

Mitt. Why is it that he's not done, and is not doing *anything*, in the private paradigm? He does nothing until/unless he becomes the head of . . .*the government*??? Remember, the Bush tax cuts which Mitt wants to retain *in toto*, have been in place *"providing tax relief and incentive for business investment to grow our economy"* . . . for how long? Part of Bush thru almost 4 years of Obama. Where are the jobs?? There ought to be jobs. But I see only clowns.

Except for increased drilling off- and onshore (including wildlife refuges), where will all the jobs come from? Back from? Will that be it? "Re-shoring" of manufacturing and assembling and all to America's shores? China and so many other countries have become co-dependent on globalism-as-détente (as well as their in**tra**-national security-through-employment plus prosperity to some extent apportioned to keep their populations peaceful). Even if we could pull back our jobs to our population, might our position be worsened by depriving, devaluing, depressing, even desecrating these other populations?

Might our national security become far less secure, because having lost what they were reciprocating with us, what would other countries (or their terrorist proxies) have to lose by attacking us?

Or would those then literally starving (because peasantry is passe as possibility for all in those lands) . . .would they respect us for assuming self-sufficiency and ceasing sinful, socialistic *"global distribution of jobs, thus survival paradigm?"*

As for China stealing? Yes, no doubt espionage and "pirating" and Intel. Prop. theft goes on. But by the cheap labor there (and in all those other countries), the corporations of here not only sell more (because they can sell cheap), but the profits percolate up into dividends and exorbitant remunerations.

But since we can't put millions to work drilling or pipe-fitting . . .

Unto Walmart (and Apple and you-name-it-everything-else), Mitt saith, *"Thou shalt bring thy jobs back to America. And thou shalt pay thy people here enough that they can maintain their life- and indulgence/purchase-style and consume great quantities of pumped productivity!!!"*

Aside from it's being also impossible, it would be consumer-sided self-destructive were he to offer as incentive to the Prodigal Sons of Corporate Cavorting abroad . . . ."*If thee return to thy home and honor thy family [domestic labor] I'll make it so it doesn't cost you any more than you're paying over there."*

Yeah, maybe   some corporations would come on home (likely only if the government paid for the relocation costs) -- except that the wages wouldn't be sufficient for the consumers could pay for the production . . .

picture that Escher drawing of two hands kind of drawing each other.
Now picture the hands holding, not pencils inscribing, but erasers . . . .
Get it?? As it "depicts" what would happen to the economy??

Regarding: (from the article)
Faith or True Religion -- "men who fear God" and a couple other items
I'll make a couple comments.
"April 2008 -- Obama speaks disrespectfully of Christians, saying they 'cling to guns or religion' and have an 'antipathy to people who are not like them'."
Obama was not speaking of Christians; rather, a segment or demographic thereof which just might include some Catholics (which in any other context the "Christians" so offended by Obama's statement . . .wouldn't consider as "Christian"). Obama was not demeaning Christianity. Nor can it be presumed that his sole focus was on gun-owning or religiousness.
  Included in his referent-group were not well-off, religious people (maybe we could include that, Cheney . . .and many others of the high-end   who not only hunt, but collect "precious weapons" and go on safaris plus to church!!
  He was, very inadvisedly, pointing out a demographic that <u>does have antipathy towards people who are not like them,</u> and for whom just being armed (with bullets or Bible) seems to be essential *raison d'etre*, if not metabolism!!
  April 2009 . . . Jesus's name was covered when he (Obama) was making a speech
  Possibly this was a factor of Homeland Security? Think about that! Those in the murderous parts of the world watch TV too. Would it really be wise to "visually conflate" the faith of the Crusaders (even recent -- as seen by them) with the President of a supposedly church-and-state-separate nation? For what purpose what would appear a flaunt or provocation, if not identifying the nation's head with a religion they hold as Satanic? Is the icon, the emblem, the logo, the symbol, so much required? So sacred? What about the heart and soul of the self (selves) of Christian believers as sufficient? Or is the symbol, a depiction, more sacred to the sensitive (kind of like representations of "the Prophet" to those others . . .)?
  The insinuation that Obama is a Muslim-in-disguise is absurd. That he belonged to Rev. Wright's rabid-sermoned church is because, though mixed-race, Barack associates himself with "black", and blacks are into that kind of fire and brimstone ("an' we suffered it personally heaped upon us during slavery") displacement? (no, *catharsis*) of "race-heritage-rage". (After slavery ended, KKK and lynchings and Jim Crow continued,

the lynching not legislatively ended until, I believe, the 1950s. So Christian and in all ways virtuous this land of the free-for-all freedom-fight for so long. Interesting, the Southern Democrats for a long time blocked attempts to pass legislation against lynching!!

February 2012 - apologizing for Koran burnings was at least a wise attempt (although it doesn't seem the apology was really accepted by the apologizee), the rabid, rampant, Muslim "street". Here was again, perhaps another nuance of not only homeland security, but for <u>our</u> "those-over-there", an attempted amelioration of situation -- by trying to calm psychotic reaction of the "native" those there.

That we burn Bibles here? Well, (Escher, above was the first), let's look at a second very convolute comparison, perhaps inside-out analogy. In other countries people burn our flag. Though we don't rampage, we get very upset. (Our burning their Korans seemed to them like their burning our flag to us. Kind of equal but opposite offended -- despite the drastically different degree of response.) But consider that in official flag-protocol, we burn "retired" flags. And, I've learned from this article, Bibles. We approve. No problem.

But where there is such out-of-control syndrome as Islamophrenia?
Obama offered an apology for offending their faith.
What's wrong with that?
Seems more Christian than not doing so.
A mere gesture, in part to subdue threat to our personnel abroad.
Barack said, "sorry" . . . to a "them" . . .
Jesus even invoked God's forgiveness of . . . another . . . . "them" .

Homosexuality has always been, will always be. There was a time when it posed a national threat. Sexuality/reproduction represented the organic-military-industrial complex (human reproduction -- of males). Engaging in sex taking time and energy-consuming, but yielding no product (boy-babies to become soldiers eventually) compromised the MIC. (the time mentioned was Biblical historic eras).
Another factor for the hetero-fixation was transmission of personal bloodlines and property through progeny. Procreation was priority over pleasurable permutations.

Homosexual "infrastructure" is an organic inherent. All creatures (that includes humans) are <u>conceived</u> female. Only after a period of cell-differentiating gestation, a binary dynamic of chromosomal "hardware" -- and hormonal-chemical "software" (uterine and circulatory milieu) -- does the unborn "potential" proceed (although there are exceptions) as actualized male or female gender, at least as obvious overt morphology of genitalia and inside repro organs.

Homosexual as "infra-chemical" being? Male and female both have male and female hormones, the proportions (testosterone, estrogen, and others) quite variable. Despite morphologically indisputable one-or-the-other-ness, the level (including "proprioception" of one's maleness or femaleness) can vary, be ambivalent, bi, or homo.

Whichever and whatever, is there not something else in the Bible about God being the one to judge, Judgment (ultimate) being up to HIM? If enacting homosexuality a sin of life-style choice, God will not only have to punish an awful lot of people (including some prominent evangelists and we won't mention priests) . . . . but other species. For homosexual behavior occurs all through the various forms of life, specially "created", . . .or through God's most comprehensive and amazing special creation -- evolution's miraculous materialization of God's *system*.

As for homosexual marriage? That someone would fear it might lead the otherwise heterosexual person away from male-and-female union . . . maybe that's someone's subconscious recognition of *his* inherent potential . . . . . historical perspective reveals, "hardly". Man and woman will mate. The while, there may be all kinds of combinations and permutations. But marriage is not under threat. Nor will youth be converted-*subverted-perverted* to homo-lifestyle. Homosexuality is not a religion let alone cult.

But I do not approve of homosexual "marriage". From the basis of keeping the language from being at least *diverted*. "Marriage" has meant man and woman for eons. So keep it that way and get another term for the love, caring, creating, exploring, existing . . of man-man or woman-woman . . . **unions**.

Thus, a why not for "marriage" . . . somewhat analogous (oh my god, here I go again), to a why not for Blacks achieving equality but clamoring that that's not good enough. "We don't just want equal rights. We want to be called Caucasians!"

And why would anyone want to use the term "Marriage?" Such a fallible institution (almost 1/3 fail within the first six years, I believe. Heterosexual marriages. Hardly sacred, "til-death-do-us-part perpetuity!!!

I do agree with a few points in the article regarding rights of religious decisions.

Hiring and health matters -- some decisions should not be superimposed. Along with the right to privacy there should be the right to priorities: even in some cases discriminatory. Catholic hospitals should not have to deal with contraception, let alone anything abortive. Certain organizations should not have to provide equal-opportunity to unwanted beliefs or orientations (although we see how uneffective even the Boy Scouts have been in self-regulating prohibitions of anyone homosexual from their Physically Pure and Morally Straight organization. But failure to achieve doesn't justify subjection to superimpositions usurping *intentions*. Some places the government does need to back-off.

Finally I come to . . . life

Protestant lifers propound that life begins at conception.

Catholic doctrine, however, starts a bit earlier and considers that *preventing* conception is sin!!

But aren't they a little late in the system of reproductive components?

Wouldn't male nocturnal emissions be . . . sins? Partial-murder? Pre-penetration abortion?

And, of course, menstruation destroys ovum (sometimes -a). SIN!!

All the uproar and outcry about the unborn, the pre-conscious (even if "*sentient*", a state prior to agony's affliction) such as . . .

starvation . . . . .
        disease . . . . . .
                sexual slavery to lunatic warlords. . . . .
                        potential recruits in their thousands, the
                        orphans of Africa, for organization by
                        Alqaida)

www.ingramcontent.com/pod-product-compliance
Lightning Source LLC
Chambersburg PA
CBHW081239180526
45171CB00005B/473